THE CULTURAL CONSTRUCTION OF RACE

Edited by
Marie de Lepervanche and Gillian Bottomley

The Cultural Construction of Race
Sydney Studies in Society and Culture, No 4

© 1988 Sydney Association for Studies in Society and Culture,
University of Sydney, NSW, Australia, 2006

National Library of Australia
Cataloguing-in-publication entry:

The Cultural construction of race.

Includes bibliographies.
ISBN 0 949405 04 3.

1. Racism. 2. Racism - Australia. 3.
Australia - Race relations. I.
De Lepervanche, Marie M. II. Bottomley,
Gillian, 1939-   . III. Sydney Association
for Studies in Society and Culture. (Series :
Sydney studies in society & culture; no. 4).

305.8

ISSN 0812-6402

Typeset and printed by *Meglamedia*, 6A Nelson St, Annandale 2038,
Phone (02) 519 1044, Fax (02) 550 3090

CONTENTS

Barker, Phil

Is a post-graduate student in the Department of General Philosophy, University of Sydney.

Bottomley, Gillian

Is an Associate Professor, Department of Anthropology and Comparative Sociology, Macquarie University.

Cowlishaw, Gillian

Is a Lecturer, School of Social Science, Mitchell College of Advanced Education, Bathurst.

Crouch, Mira

Is a Senior Lecturer, School of Sociology, University of New South Wales.

Kalantzis, Mary

Is a Research Fellow at the Centre for Multicultural Studies, University of Wollongong.

Lechte, John

Is a Lecturer, Department of Sociology, School of Behavioural Sciences, Macquarie University.

de Lepervanche, Marie

Is an Associate Professor, Department of Anthropology, University of Sydney.

Lovric, Barbara

Is a post-graduate student, Department of Indonesian and Malayan Studies, University of Sydney.

Markus, Andrew

Is a Lecturer in History, Monash University.

Miles, Robert

Is a Lecturer in Sociology, University of Glasgow.

Introduction

Marie de Lepervanche and Gillian Bottomley

In the wake of the 'Blainey debate' which erupted in Australia in 1984, academics in various disciplines have been preoccupied with both continuities and discontinuities in our thinking about race over the last two centuries. Another topic of more popular public concern is the forthcoming bicentenary of white settlement in Australia which, to Aboriginal people, is hardly cause for celebration at all, given their experience of conquest and racism since 1788. These were some of the reasons why the Sydney Association for Studies in Society and Culture held a conference on The Cultural Construction of Race in August 1985. This collection offers some of the papers to a wider readership. Although the immediate interests of contributors range over topics as diverse as eighteenth century voyages in the Pacific to Hitler's *Mein Kampf,* there are common threads linking their concerns; these include the implications for western culture of constructing the 'imagined communities' of race and nation, and the consequences for non-western others of these historical constructions of the body and the body politic.

For earlier generations, the biological foundations for race differences were incontrovertible and these 'natural' bodily distinctions were believed to parallel the observed differences between cultural achievements in the 'civilised' and not-so-civilised world. During European hegemony over colonial possessions in the 19th century, empirical observation and scientific experiment 'proved' the inferiority of other races and legitimated their subjugation. Hitler's Germany carried this kind of thinking and practice to its genocidal conclusion. After the second World War we seemed for a while to have buried race and racism as an extraordinary amount of international labour migration throughout the western world, often from former colonies, produced physically and culturally heterogeneous populations in many western nation states. Guest workers in Europe, black immigrants in Britain and southern Europeans and Asians in Australia entered the hosts' workforces, often in low status jobs where their labour was needed. Their increasing visibility, particularly after recession began in the early 1970s, elicited the host response that they, the immigrants, were social problems.

In Australia, according to Blainey, there are too many Asians entering at a time when jobs are short: their customs are not like ours and this dif-

1

ference poses a threat to the Australian way of life. Immigration policy should therefore take note of the ordinary Australian's concern for this cultural disruption, attendant upon the Vietnamese refugee intake particularly, and the nation should look more to its traditional sources of migration, for example the United Kingdom, for future settlers. Our family reunion scheme, in Blainey's words, is a racial reunion scheme and if we are not careful Australia will become an Asian nation unless significant changes with respect to immigration are made (Blainey, 1984).

In this way of thinking, race, culture and nation are conflated. Yet, the crude racism of the nineteenth century and of Hitler's Reich, when Europeans equated phenotype with cultural superiority/ inferiority, is not publicly condoned today. Even the biologists have rejected race as a legitimate scientific category. But a 'new racism' has emerged in which physical and cultural differences are accepted as natural and the argument proceeds from an acceptance of a human nature which we all share (Cf. Barker, 1981). Thus, it is human nature to cleave to one's own kind, one's culture and one's nation. The rationalisations for excluding those who look different or who are culturally unlike us, then, does not directly appeal to old fashioned notions of race but to ideas about an allegedly universal human nature that is nepotistic and which seeks to preserve its own national way of life.

In both the United Kingdom and Australia, where populations are now both ethnically/ 'racially' heterogeneous, Enoch Powell and Geoffrey Blainey respectively appeal to an ethnic/ 'racial' homogeneity to ensure social cohesion. Their arguments ignore the structural inequalities of class as well as differences in social power between various other segments of the population, for example, gender divisions. Even so, this prescription for cohesion and social harmony makes common sense to some people; while local Australians compete for jobs with 'ethnics', and Australian children compete for university places with Asians who work hard and win entry to tertiary institutions, and while new arrivals who look different from us live in hostels located in areas of high immigrant settlement, then, physical difference and cultural divisions are easily held up as the sources of social anxiety about threats to our national way of life. Blainey's intervention tends to legitimate these fears and, despite all the rhetoric of multiculturalism, the possibility of a constantly changing Australian culture, or cultures, is ignored. The quest for homogeneous identity also excludes the Aboriginal presence.

The rejection of race as a biological category notwithstanding, for some Europeans and Australians white superiority is a fact of life. After all, Europe had its colonies until recently and many Australians grew up with a 'White' Australia policy that lasted into the 1960s. Insofar as there has been an historical process of reifying race in European and Australian discourse since the 19th century, the idea of race continues to inform our common sense even though the terms we use may have changed. This process of racialisation, as Robert Miles (this volume) calls it, remains a powerful ideological device that inheres in the political life of Britain and Australia.

The academic reaction to Blainey nevertheless has tended to be critical, particularly the historians' comments which have extended to Blainey's earlier work on Aboriginal occupation of the continent as well as covering his more recent publications (Cf. Markus and Ricklefs, 1985). Some Australian social scientists are also exploring this field of the 'new racism' in commentaries on Aboriginal social life and through critical analyses of 'ethnicity' and 'multiculturalism' as explanatory concepts (Cf. Cowlishaw and Kalantzis, this volume: Bottomley and de Lepervanche, 1984). The influence of contemporary philosophical debates is also apparent in the work of other scholars who consider the power of language/ knowledge in directing the course of debate about the 'other', and in constructing categories of thought, such as race, culture and nation, in which the 'other' has a subordinate place (Cf. Barker and Lechte, this volume). All take issue with the Blainey view and with those who posit, implicitly or explicitly, a human nature that makes ethnocentrism and/ or racism 'natural' and inevitable. All share the common problem, as well, of theorising the predicament created by the construction of these 'imagined communities'; for even while struggling out of one paradigm in which race, culture and biology are equated, we invariably use language and terms inappropriate to our new theoretical perspectives!

Given that British academic enterprise has produced a distinct field of race relations sociology which, in turn, has been appropriated by British administrative practice with respect to Indian and Afro-Caribbean immigrants to the United Kingdom, we are fortunate to have Robert Miles' contribution because he scrutinises the reification of race in British commonsense notions about black immigrants and looks critically at the race relations industry itself. In the process, Miles questions his academic colleagues and the consequences of their theories; he also charts the racialisation of British political discourse over the last quarter century, during which time black immigrants provided much of the unskilled and semiskilled labour for British industry. While examining Enoch Powell's contribution in shifting the direction of this discourse from an explicit emphasis on race and immigration in the 1950s to an accent on nation and repatriation in the 1960s, Miles demonstrates the historical connection between British nationalism and racism. For Australians, whose emergent nationalism with Federation in 1901 was so clearly grounded in a racism that excluded non-Europeans and denigrated the Aboriginal inhabitants of

3

the continent, there are familiar echoes here. There are also lessons to be learnt both from a comparison between British and Australian experiments with immigration, and from understanding the way Enoch Powell legitimated commonsense notions of race in articulating a theory of nationalism that evoked the Englishman's (sic) 'natural' affection for the British way of life and his 'natural' desire to defend it from the 'alien' threat.

In John Lechte's contribution we first go back to the eighteenth century to consider both the antecedents of our modern conceptions of race, especially insofar as they were generated by the voyages of colonial exploration in the Pacific, and the discontinuities between an earlier ethnocentrism and the more modern forms of racism. Lechte's essay raises the general problem of the European's representation of the 'other' and its limitations. Drawing on Foucault, Lechte discusses how the interrelation between the development of nineteenth and twentieth century state power (compared with the sovereign power of eighteenth century absolute monarchies) and biology have had particular consequences for populations and their surveillance. These consequences include both the construction of 'races' and their destruction through genocide.

A preoccupation with surveillance and with bodily differences within its population has characterised the rather blundering attempts by Australian governments over the last 199 years to order and control the Aboriginal people. In his survey of the Australian use of racial concepts in legislation and as governmental statistical categories, Andrew Markus shows how race and nation have been conflated, as have race and culture, both with respect to discourses about Aborigines and in recent legislation purporting to outlaw racism. The Racial Discrimination Act 1975, for instance, presents a paradox in that categories like race, colour and ethnic / national origin are lumped together at the same time as the legislation tries to remove or make illegal the pejorative evaluations attached to them.

Notwithstanding the intent of legislation designed to be anti-racist, the circumstances that many Aboriginal people find themselves in today testify to continuing white racism in this country. Gillian Cowlishaw's essay addresses this issue through a commentary on the silences about racism-as-a-problem in a number of anthropological characterisations of Aboriginal culture. Although a version of her paper has appeared in an anthropological journal, the version given at the Conference and which appears here is included in the hope that it reaches a readership that is interdisciplinary. Cowlishaw recalls nineteenth century notions of race and explores the way in which these continue to inform, if only implicitly, current ideas of cultural difference between various kinds of contemporary Aboriginal people. She refers to continuities in commonsense notions

4

about 'real' Aborigines in the north of the continent and the black urban dwellers of the south, and specifically addresses the anthropological construction of traditional Aboriginal culture as distinctive of northern areas of Australia and now allegedly gone or destroyed in the south. This north/south distinction, according to Cowlishaw, implicitly relies on theories of culture that draw on nineteenth century notions of race, despite explicit rejections of the latter. Such theories also fail to credit Aboriginal people with resisting white domination to the extent that they have, or with their capacity to construct new and different cultures from their experiences of domination and disadvantage after white conquest.

Focusing on other segments in the Australian population who have also experienced ethnocentrism or racism, Mary Kalantzis attempts in her essay to deconstruct the racism embedded in Multicultural policy and practice in the educational field. She argues that as schooling in Australia is compulsory until children reach the age of fifteen years, educational institutions are crucial sites for socialisation and that multiculturalism, despite its rhetoric of understanding other cultures and the politics of difference, implicates the old notion of race (and hence social inequality) while trying to reject earlier racisms. Kalantzis suggests an alternative teaching programme for schools in the Social Literacy Project which provides room for both celebrating cultural diversity and recognising the structural inequalities of class and the associated disadvantages immigrants are implicated in. This Project is designed specifically to empower children and their teachers to understand these inequalities and to intervene actively in their own lives and self-creation.

Another kind of social inequality is the major concern of de Lepervanche's paper, namely, gender inequality and the complex interrelation between nationalism, racism and sexism in Australian society. She briefly considers the extent to which racism and nationalism, and the institution of the family with which both are often associated, affect men and women differently. She argues that the intersection of class, race and gender inequalities provide women with a particular kind of social disadvantage that is rarely mentioned in the literature. Yet in nineteenth century Australia, and also since the introduction of non-Anglophone immigrants since World War II, both racist and sexist ideologies have flourished in public evaluations and representations of the nation and the family.

The representation of woman as sexual object, together with other images of race and gender, are the topics of Mira Crouch's essay on Puccini's 'Madam Butterfly'. Considered as a metaphor, Butterfly in her kimono, 'singing her heart out', becomes the 'quintessential female figure'. Crouch's thesis is that in this opera Puccini transforms a racial (and gender) stereotype into an archetype. Drawing on information about Puccini's

5

lifelong preoccupation with women and their voices, Crouch argues that his objectification of Butterfly continues to 'speak to' audiences today.

Barbara Lovric's contribution looks to the colonial experience and after in Indonesia, and to the construction by various writers of 'culturally induced' mental illness among its population. Formerly, Europeans tended to consider many of these diseases to be the result of 'racial' pre-dispositions, but in more recent years cultural rather than racial stereotyping has become more common. In criticism of this trend to arraign a people's culture, Lovric suggests that some of the indigenous medical classifications invite greater attention and that tropical neurology has a lot to learn about exotic 'mental disorders'. As Lovric also notes, the politics of medical research tend to direct efforts towards lengthening the lives of affluent people instead of concentrating on the impoverished or less well off populations.

In the final paper of the volume, in which Phil Barker contemplates the silences in philosophical discourse concerning Hitler's *Mein Kampf,* some of the themes addressed in other papers recur. The exclusion of *My Struggle* from works commonly classified as 'philosophical' and the untranslatability of the title (we know it best in German), suggests to Barker that for English speakers, at least, the book and its author's practices are totally alien to our own. Yet, as Barker points out, *Mein Kampf* is part of the European cultural heritage and needs to be seriously addressed as such. Neither fascism nor racism is exclusive to Hitler's Reich.

Another theme Barker considers is the overcoming of namelessness in Hitler's rise to power, and the search for an identity that draws on a past cultural history that is continuous with the present. The achievements of a glorious past are thus used to construct the homogeneous 'pure' who belong to the group and to exclude the 'other'. This theme recalls Enoch Powell's reference to the Englishman's instinct for continuity and his desire to keep the 'alien' from sharing in the British nation (cf. Miles this volume; Barker, 1981: 21-22, 32, 39).

In multicultural Australia we may think Enoch Powell's arguments for repatriating black immigrants are irrelevant to us, but Barker reminds us that our preparations for bicentennial celebrations are not without a search for origins, an identity and for continuities. It is as well to remember the Aboriginal experience of discontinuity and domination.

Beyond the 'Race' Concept: The Reproduction of Racism in England

Robert Miles

Large numbers of people continue for long periods of time to cling to myth, to justify it in formulas that are repeated in their cultures, and to reject falsifying information when prevailing myths justify their interests, roles, and past actions, or assuage their fears. (Edelman, 1977:3)

The deepest instinct of the Englishman - how the word 'instinct' keeps forcing itself in again and again! - is for continuity: he never acts more freely nor innovates more boldly than when he is conscious of conserving or even of reacting (Enoch Powell, cited in Wood, 1965:145)

This is the doctrine of the new tribalism, and as such would make sure, if it prevailed, that there would be Washingtons and riots in Britain. (*Times,* 18.11.67)

Introduction

This paper has two objectives. First, it will summarise and develop my critique of the sociology of 'race relations' and the way in which it utilises the idea of 'race' as an analytical concept. It will be concluded from this that it is necessary to show why and how the idea of 'race' is employed in social relations rather than take for granted its commonsense status. The concepts of racialisation and racism will be shown to be central to this task. Second, as a way of illustrating the significance of this argument, I shall consider a key phase in the racialisation of domestic English politics. I show, first, how the 1964/70 Labour government initially employed the idea of 'race' to problematise the migrant presence in favour of the exposure of racism and, second, how Enoch Powell subverted a later attempt to do the latter by an ideological intervention which employed the category of 'nation' as an allusion to the idea of 'race'.

The Ideological Character of 'Race Relations' Sociology

A confrontation with the idea of 'race' is a confrontation with the history and legacy of a central strand of Western thought. During the late eighteenth and the nineteenth centuries, the idea of 'race' occupied a key place in the attempt by intellectuals and politicians to understand the rapidly changing and expanding world in which they lived, and the successful attempt to attribute scientific status to the idea of 'race' is now well understood (Banton, 1977). That some eight million people had to die in the course of a political project influenced by that bogus science is also well understood, despite ongoing attempts by fascist groups to define this historical episode as a myth. The work of many biologists and geneticists both before and after the Holocaust has demonstrated, clearly and repeatedly, that the idea of there being discrete biological groups ranged in a hierarchy of superiority/ inferiority has no scientific foundation. Ambiguities remain in the way in which some of them continue to employ the idea of 'race' within scientific discourse but where its use is maintained and defended, it is in terms which are clearly divorced from the nineteenth century emphasis upon the classification of phenotypical variation (Montagu, 1972). 'Race', in the sense of discrete sub-species, is no longer seriously considered to be biological fact. Thus 'any use of racial categories must take its justifications from some other source than biology' (Rose et. al., 1984:127).

Most social scientists accept and adopt this as their starting point when analysing the continuing reproduction of racism. But, in the course of rejecting scientific racism, many of them have incorporated the key 'concept' of scientific racism into their analytical framework. They have redefined 'race' as a social category and utilise it as both explanans and explanandum, in an attempt to constitute 'race relations' as a discrete object of analysis, about which theories can be formulated, tested and reformulated (e.g. Rex, 1970; cf. Miles, 1982, 1984b).

Historically, and in the contemporary world, people attribute meaning to particular patterns of phenotypical variation and act in accordance with that process of signification. The occurrence of this complex process of cognition and action is not contested. What is contested is the analytical method and concepts employed to understand and explain it. The conventional sociological method is to claim that, as a result of this process, 'races' are constituted and thereby come to relate to one another, and that the means and consequences of this fall into regular patterns which can be theorised. Thereafter, and crucially, 'race' is transformed into a real phenomenon which has identifiable effects in the social world. 'Race' becomes a variable with measurable consequences. Sociologists employ this variable to report that, for example, 'race' has important effects on educational achievement, that 'race' interrelates with class to produce multiple patterns of disadvantage, that 'race' intervenes in the political process affecting the way in which people vote, that 'race' determines an individual's chances of being unemployed, arrested by the police or becoming a magistrate, and so on. That is, sociologists employ the idea of 'race' as an explanans, as an analytical concept identifying a phenomenon with determinant effects.

This is a classic example of reification. There is no identifiable phenomenon of 'race' which can have such effects on social relations and processes. There is only a process of signification in the course of which the idea of 'race' is employed to interpret the presence and behaviour of others, a conceptual process which can guide subsequent action and reaction. This complex of signification and action, where it occurs systematically over periods of time, has structural consequences. This complex can be referred to as a process of racialisation, a concept which refers to the social construction but also refers to patterns of action and reaction consequent upon the signification. Within this process, the ideology of racism plays a central role by offering criteria upon which signification can occur, attributing negative correlates to all those possessing the real or alleged criteria, and legitimating consequent discriminatory behaviour or consequences.

This 'race relations' sociology takes for granted and legitimates commonsense definitions. This point was made in a review over fifteen years ago of a text by one of Britain's foremost exponents of 'race relations' sociology where it was argued that:

> One cannot avoid the suspicion that Banton's concept of race is simply the popular British concept shorn of its innuendos of prejudice and raised from the daily life of the British Isles to the status of a universal scientific category (Pitt-Rivers, 1970:340).

In other words, it assumes something that needs to be explained. Put yet another way, the reality of phenotypical variation is usually regarded as an adequate explanation of signification. But not all phenotypical differences are interpreted as evidence for the supposed existence of 'race'. The human species can be classified into categories by a very wide range of phenotypical features (e.g. size of feet, eye colour, hair colour, height etc.) but only a limited range tends to be referred to as signifying 'race' (e.g. skin colour). Therefore, there is an ongoing process of ideological construction and re-construction which requires explanation.

This claim is reinforced by the historical fact that not all instances of social relations between individuals categorised as being of distinct 'race' are followed by the mutual reproduction of the signification in practice. The scientific racism of the nineteenth century had such a pervasive influence that almost all instances of group differentiation were liable to be interpreted in terms of 'race'. For example, Elizabeth Gaskell's biography of Charlotte Bronte refers to the population of Yorkshire as a 'race' and outlines their supposedly distinctive cultural characteristics (1975:60). More significantly, Irish migrants to Scotland in the nineteenth century were identified as a 'race' and were subjected to violent physical attack and systematic discrimination (Miles, 1982:121-50). Yet, in neither case have the process and consequences been signified either by the participants or sociologists as a 'race relations' situation.

The attribution of the categories of 'race' and 'race relations' is, therefore, an ideological process which occurs in particular circumstances. Its occurrence requires explanation because

> ... language is an integral facet of the political scene; not simply an instrument for describing events but itself a part of events, shaping their meaning and helping to shape the political roles officials and the general public play. In this sense, language, events, and self-conceptions are a part of the same transaction, mutually determining one another's meanings (Edelman, 1977:4).

The signification of an individual as belonging to a 'race' or of a situation as being one of 'race relations' is an event which has particular consequences because

> ... Perception involves categorisation. To place an object in one class of things rather than another establishes its central characteristics and creates assumptions about matters that are not seen (Edelman, 1977:23).

It is also an event which has certain preconditions which need to be identified and explained.

A further reason for rejecting 'race relations' sociology follows from the key place that the idea of 'race' occupies in Western commonsense (understood in the Gramscian sense). The reification of the process of signification and the attribution of analytical status to the idea of 'race' transforms the phenotypical feature into a determining agent, reproducing at another level the causal sequence which scientific racism purported to identify. Thus, 'race' is transformed from being an idea employed in a process of signification into an active subject in the same manner that scientific racism asserted that a complex of phenotypical characteristics determined social processes and outcomes. 'Race relations' sociology denies this determining process but articulates an analytical sequence in which it is echoed and reincarnated. This consequence of reification is particularly problematic when 'race relations' sociology reports its findings and conclusions to politicians, the media and the public in a historical context in which the nineteenth century idea of 'race' continues to be reproduced. In such circumstances, the process of reification confirms and legitimates the historically constituted commonsense notion that 'race' is a biological fact with determinant effects. Thus, 'race relations' sociology plays a role in the legitimation of commonsense ideas about 'race' and, consequently, remains on the same ideological terrain as the racist. Viewed in this context, the incorporation of such an ideological notion into sociological analysis is a political act and needs to be consistently exposed as such.

One crucial consequence is that the ideas of 'race' and 'race relations' are used in a way which obscures historical and social processes. In asserting that a 'race relations' problem exists, it is implied that the development of social interaction between the different 'races' constitutes the origin of the problem. Thus, when West Indians migrated to England in the 1950s, it was claimed that their arrival and presence created a 'race relations' problem. This formulation is ideological because it locates the origin of what is defined as problematic in the very presence of the migrant group. Such an interpretation reverses the sequence of events and obscures the active agent in the process. The determining signification and action is the initial definition of the migrants as a distinct 'race' whose presence is denoted as creating a 'race relations' problem. 'Race relations' are not naturally occurring relations between 'races' but is a label applied to situations in which the participants are defined and define themselves as 'races'. The determining factor is, therefore, the act of definition and the action taken to reinforce and sustain that definition. By obscuring this process, the influence of racism itself can be downgraded or ignored when it is often this ideology which sustains that initial act of categorisation.

The Historical Character of 'Race Relations' Sociology

Although the idea of 'race' has had a lengthy genesis in European thought, it was during the late eighteenth and the nineteenth centuries that scientists, intellectuals and politicans posed the problem of explaining 'race relations' and found an answer in biology (cf. Miles, 1982:43). It was not until the early twentieth century that sociological forms of analysis began to appropriate the same object but shift certain of the analytical categories while retaining the idea of 'race' as an analytical concept. This first occurred in the United States with the publication of *Introduction to the Science of Society* by R. Park and E.W. Burgess in 1921. Subsequently, during the 1920s and 1930s, a sociological tradition defined and analysed 'race relations' as socially-defined relations and produced a series of classic investigations which focused in particular on the southern states of the USA (Richmond, 1969:238: Banton, 1977:101-35).

This first sociology of 'race relations' identified such relations as an internal problem within the United States at a time when the migration of a section of the American population of African origin from the southern to the northern states was under way (Piore, 1979:143, 157-63). This migration of labour had its origin in a particular phase of capital accumulation in the United States, during which an addition to the ranks of the unskilled and semi-skilled industrial proletariat was required in the northern centres of capitalist production. The migration was possible because of the uneven character of capitalist development which had left large sections of the population in the southern states in considerable poverty. A part of that section of the population of African origin which had earlier been racialised in the course of establishing, legitimating and reproducing the slave mode of production was then summoned by capital to reconstitute its relation to the capitalist mode of production by selling labour power for a wage. A period of marginalisation and externalisation was ended as these Afro-Americans were encouraged to occupy a pivotal position at the heart of the process of extraction of surplus value. It was in response to this historical process that sociologists in the USA laid the foundations for 'race relations' sociology.

A similar process occurred in Britain. Although there were small communities of colonial origin in Britain in the nineteenth century, as well as a large migrant population from Ireland, all of which had been racialised and subject to physical attack, their presence was neither politically identified as constituting a 'race relations' problem nor considered by the infant social sciences as worthy of attention. It was only following the economically induced migration of labour from the Caribbean and the Indian subcontinent during the 1950s that such a definition was applied and such attention was given. This work tended to borrow heavily from the American tradition.

'Race relations' sociology can therefore be viewed as an attempt to confront the problem of racism when historically racialised populations are transferred from the colonial periphery to the centre of the world system of commodity production to be proletarianised. It constitutes an attempt to analyse a real problem which highlights certain central contradictions in the reproduction of capitalist relations of production. Increasingly, it has become necessary for the state to intervene to manage the conflicts that arise from the reproduction of racism in the metropolitan centre, and 'race relations' sociology, because of its ideological character, can be appropriated and utilised as part of the project of containment (Gilroy, 1980). By understanding the essential relations that underlie the origin of 'race relations' sociology, it is possible to employ a more adequate analytical framework within which to locate the process of racialisation (cf. Miles, 1982:94-133). In what follows, I focus in some detail on a particular phase in the racialisation of domestic English politics and in the conclusion I briefly relate this to economic relations.

The Racialisation of Politics in England in the 1950s
The most cursory examination of political history in England since 1945 reveals that only a minority of participants in formal political processes

have articulated openly a racist theory which approximates to the claims of the biological sciences in the nineteenth century. There is, therefore, a sense in which Banton was correct to assert that racism is dead (1970:28), at least in the English context. But the validity of this assertion is contradicted by two considerations. First, small fascist parties have continued since 1945 to articulate the central claims of scientific racism, and these parties have had, in certain periods, a significant influence on the political process (cf. Miles & Phizacklea, 1984:113-35). Second, there is a debate about the definition and nature of racism, and different definitions admit different criteria as a measure of the presence or persistence of the ideology (Miles, 1982:72-92). Such conceptual debates are important, but do not in themselves solve the problem if they are abstracted from the historical and contemporary evidence. In what follows, my primary concern is with some of that evidence.

I now approach that evidence in the light of the analytical and conceptual implications of the preceding argument. My claim is that the articulation of racism in English politics is more clearly revealed if we first appreciate that the idea of 'race' is a central component of national commonsense. This assertion presumes a historical relationship between racism and nationalism in the English case which cannot be pursued in detail here. It is sufficient to note that the idea of 'race' occupied a central role in the writing of English history (Banton, 1977:15-26; MacDougall, 1982) and was employed by all classes of the English population during the nineteenth century in order to comprehend the populations of those parts of the world which had been or were to be incorporated into the British Empire. As an element of commonsense, the idea of 'race' need not necessarily be explicitly articulated for it to have real effects on the political process. By definition, commonsense is all those 'taken for granted' ideas and 'facts' which shape the manner in which problems are defined and solutions sought. This can be done without the idea of 'race' ever being articulated. And even when the idea of 'race' is explicitly articulated, its commonsense status ensures that such usage does not require legitimation or explanation.

During the 1950s, 'race' was constructed as an object of political debate in England and as a problem requiring political intervention. The concept of racialisation refers to this historical process of reifying the idea of 'race', of conceiving it as a real object. Brittan and Maynard express the consequences in the following way:

> ... political discourse proceeds as if the reality 'race' was self-evident. Parliament legislates on 'race'. The media discuss 'race'. Politicians discover 'race' as an important dimension of their appeal to the electorate (1984:13).

The sociology of 'race relations' takes this for granted and subsequently legitimates this ideological process by proceeding to offer an explanation which accepts that there is a 'race' problem in England. I wish to problematise what is 'taken-for-granted' and ask why it is that the arrival of people in England from the Caribbean and the Indian subcontinent was interpreted using the idea of 'race'.

This requires historical reconstruction in order to explain the context for and the means by which 'race' entered English political discourse. Let us narrow that task immediately by assuming that it did so in the context of British colonialism and, therefore, that the 'race' problem was construed as being largely external to England in the period before 1945. This is an assumption which is not fully justified if we take account of, for example, the ideological reaction to the Jewish migration in the late nineteenth century or the physical attacks on people of colonial origin in English seaports in the early twentieth century (Joshua et al., 1983:7-55), but it is an assumption which does not contradict the general thesis that political intervention creates 'race' as an object of attention and action. In the post-1945 period, a migration from the Caribbean (and later from the Indian subcontinent) was stimulated by a shortage of semi- and unskilled labour in certain sectors of the English economy and proceeded by means of a politically unregulated chain migration. The ideological signification of this migration employed the idea of 'race', and this was the crucial first step in the racialisation of domestic English politics.

These Commonwealth and British subjects became the object of two contradictory political processes. The first was a process of exclusion. Discrimination was practised to limit their access to housing and places of entertainment, and this required an ideological legitimation. The second was a process of inclusion. Various forms of organisation attempted to ease and assist their entry into English social relations, and this too required ideological legitimation. Initially, neither the migration nor these reactive processes received sustained, formal and public attention by the state or individual politicians, although both had been privately engaged in various sorts of activity from the 1940s which indicated that they defined the migration as problematic (Joshi & Carter, 1984). In other words, there were a number of crosscutting political and ideological reactions to the migration within civil society, but none received public state attention in the early and mid-1950s.

The situation changed following a fight outside a pub in Nottingham and a subsequent series of attacks on West Indian migrants and their property in the summer of 1958. Similar incidents occurred in London. The events themselves matter less than the political and ideological reaction to them (cf. Miles, 1984b). The political debate following the attacks, as refracted by newspaper reporting, provides a classic example of Edelman's claim that

> Political and ideological debate consists very largely of efforts to win acceptance of a particular categorisation of an issue in the face of competing efforts of a different one ... (1977:25).

The categorisation that predominated over the several ones articulated asserted that the 'riots' demonstrated that England faced a 'race' problem as a result of 'immigration'. This categorisation had a certain phenomenal adequacy insofar as it was commonly assumed by both politicians and audience that the world's population was divided into distinct 'races' and that it was by means of 'immigration' that they came into contact with each other. I refer to this categorisation as the 'race/ immigration' dualism. As a result of its predominance, 'race' and 'immigration' were established as legitimate objects of political attention and action.

There are a number of things to note about this categorisation. First, it displaced any reference to the facts which demonstrated that the so-called 'riots' began as a result of attacks on West Indian migrants and that those who perpetrated these attacks identified their victims using categories such as 'nigger'. By defining 'race as the problem, the implicit reification obscured the social process of categorisation, with the result that the object of categorisation (and attack) was transformed into the origin of the ideologically constructed problem. Second, each pole of the dualism defined and contained the other. Hence, and third, the dualism contained both explanation and solution to the problem. By suggesting that the 'race' problem had been created by 'immigration', the solution was 'obviously' to be found in stopping 'immigration'. Finally, it served to dislocate the legal status of the settlers as United Kingdom subjects who had the right to enter and live in Britain.

The predominance of this dualism was achieved without any attempt by either leading parliamentary politicians or journalists to identify explicitly the 'immigrants' as a 'race' which exhibited undesirable and negatively evaluated biological characteristics. But some Labour and Conservative politicians did link the category 'coloured immigrants' in a deterministic manner with a number of negatively evaluated characteristics, from which they concluded that the migration of such people should be controlled. This interpretation was sanctioned by the decision of the Conservative government in 1961 to establish controls over the entry into Britain of Commonwealth citizens, controls which were not applied to citizens of the Irish Republic. The Labour Party criticised for being inspired by racism and opposed the legislation as a matter of principle. However, over the following eighteen months, there was a clear retreat from this position, principally by the Labour leadership, which became obvious following the election of a Labour government in 1964 (cf. Layton-Henry, 1984:57).

The Labour government published a White Paper in 1965 titled *Immigration from the Commonwealth* which endorsed and developed the 'race/ immigration' categorisation. It endorsed the categorisation by proposing even stricter controls over 'immigration' and developed it by proposing that the state should intervene to improve 'race relations'. The analysis offered in this official document is worthy of careful attention because of what it reveals about the Labour government's ideological construction. The document claimed to set out both a Commonwealth 'immigration policy' and a policy to deal with 'the problems to which it has given rise'. The latter was dealt with in Part III under the title 'Integration', in which the United Kingdom was described as a 'multi-racial society' in which

> ... the presence ... of nearly one million immigrants from the Commonwealth with different social and cultural backgrounds raises a number of problems and creates various social tensions in those areas where they have concentrated (HMSO, 1965:10).

It went on to claim that these problems and tensions would have to be resolved if

> ... we are to avoid the evil of racial strife and if harmonious relations between the different races who now form our community are to develop ... (HMSO, 1965:10).

Thus 'harmonious race relations' was defined as the policy goal and was to be achieved by solving the problems created by the 'immigrants'. These problems were said to have arisen in housing, education, employment and health.

Within three of these areas, the document claimed that the 'immigrant' presence was the origin of the problem. Concerning housing, it was claimed that:

> The main cause of unsatisfactory living conditions among immigrants is the multiple occupation of houses originally designed for one family (HMSO, 1965:11).

Concerning education, it was argued that

> ... most of the difficulties arise from the fact that numbers of immigrant children newly arrived from overseas are brought to school without previous warning, often knowing little or no English, and ignorant of the normal social habits and ways of life in this country (HMSO, 1965:11).

16

Part of the solution to this problem was seen to lie with dispersing these children in order to prevent their 'undue concentration'. As far as health was concerned, the document asserted that:

> The main problem presented to the local authorities is the detection and prevention of tuberculosis ... One of the main pressures that Commonwealth immigrants exert on local hospital facilities arises from the fact that their poor housing conditions are unsuitable for home confinements and that this leads to a heavy demand for hospital maternity beds (HMSO, 1965:14).

Clearly, as far as the Labour government was concerned, the main obstacle to 'harmonious race relations' was the presence and behaviour of 'immigrants'.

But there was a subsidiary and secondary theme which emerged in the discussion of employment. Here, it was noted that the majority of 'immigrants' were employed and that the only problem was the persistence of discrimination against them which was being dealt with by withholding help from employers who set discriminatory criteria in the hiring of labour and by using 'persuasion and reasoning' to overcome 'difficulties'. This was a problem in which 'considerable progress has already been made' (HMSO, 1965:13) and which therefore required no major initiative. This was echoed by a later claim that 'mutual tolerance and understanding' would be achieved because of the 'good sense of the British people' (HMSO, 1965:18). Here was the merest hint that the problem lay not with the migrants but with the reaction to them, but this suggestion immediately dismissed the assertion that action had already been taken to resolve this difficulty and that an alleged characteristic of the indigenous population necessarily limited its scope.

Although the 1965 White Paper offered no sustained argument, supported with evidence, to suggest that the problem lay with the conception and action of the indigenous population, yet, when the government intervened to legislate for 'race relations' in 1965 and 1968, it was legislation that defined racial discrimination as illegal and that sought to penalise such behaviour. Here was a clear contradiction between the way in which the government construed the nature of the problem and the action it took, although an attempt was made prior to the introduction of the 1968 legislation to legitimate it with evidence on the extent of discrimination in England (Daniel, 1968). In the light of the predominance of the 'race/ immigration' categorisation and the predominant opinion that there were 'too many immigrants in Britain' this was a difficult venture. Meanwhile, events in East Africa were encouraging the migration to Britain of Kenyan Asians holding UK passports, and a number of right-wing Conservative politicians reacted in such a way as to re-focus the political debate on the commonsense logic of the 'race/ immigration' dualism, and thereafter to offer a new categorisation.

Powell and the Racialisation of Politics

The most important member of this group of politicians was Enoch Powell MP who was Shadow Minister for Defence. In 1968 he made three speeches which dealt explicitly with 'immigration' and with the problems that he considered to have arisen from 'immigration'. In each of them, he argued that the solution to the problems that he identified lay no longer with immigration control alone but with a state organised policy of 'repatriation'. Each of the three speeches was carefully constructed and there is therefore special significance in the fact that the idea of 'race' was rarely employed. Indeed, on one of the few occasions when the 'race' idea was articulated, Powell did so in order to deny that the extent of the diversity of 'race' or culture of the 'immigrants' was problematic in itself (Smithies and Fiddick, 1969:68). This is usually ignored by academic commentators who themselves uncritically interpret Powell's speeches by using the 'race/ immigration' dualism (e.g. Layton-Henry, 1984:70-2; 75-7) and who therefore fail to grasp the ideological shift that Powell attempted in 1968 and after. Barker, too, uses a reified concept of 'race', although I agree with his analysis of Powell as a key figure in the construction of the 'new racism' (1981:37-42). Unfortunately, Barker contextualises Powell primarily in terms of Conservative party politics rather than in relation to the broader process of racialisation which is what I attempt to do here.

In the 1968 speeches, Powell's primary concern was with the alleged effects of the numbers and characteristics of the migrants upon the English people or 'nation'. This became clear, for example, in his attack in the Birmingham speech on the Race Relations Bill (which aimed to extend the provisions of the Race Relations Act, 1965, to housing and employment) which was then being discussed in Parliament. Powell argued that the English people

> ... now learn that a one way privilege is to be established by act of parliament; a law, which cannot, and is not intended, to operate to protect them or redress their grievances, is to be enacted to give the stranger, the disgruntled and the *agent provocateur* the power to pillory for them for their private actions (quoted in Smithies and Fiddick, 1969:40; cf. pp.38-9, 43).

Powell's concern was that the English, described as having 'incredible tolerance' (Smithies and Fiddick, 1969:69), would lose their right to discriminate in pursuing their rightful interests (Smithies and Fiddick, 1969:39) in a context where

> They found their wives unable to obtain hospital beds in childbirth,

their children unable to obtain schoolplaces, their homes and neighbourhoods changed beyond recognition, their plans and prospects for the future defeated ... (Smithies and Fiddick, 1969:40).

This imagery of the systematic disadvantage created for the English as a result of migration was contrasted with the limited problems faced by the migrants which, in Powell's view, arose from 'personal circumstances and accidents' (Smithies and Fiddick, 1969;40). Here Powell was denying that the migrant population was the object of systematic discrimination and disadvantage.

This alleged material disadvantage (for the English) arising from migration echoed the claims of the Labour Party's 1965 White Paper and illustrates the extent of the common ideological terrain on which the contest was occurring. But Powell took the argument a stage further. These alleged disadvantages which arose, first from the sheer size of the immigrant population were, he continued, accentuated by the wish of the immigrants to maintain their distinct cultural identity and practices. In the Eastbourne speech, he cited a sociological study of migration from the Caribbean to support this argument and went on to argue that

> Sometimes people point to the increasing proportion of immigrant offspring born in this country as if the fact contained within itself the ultimate solution. The truth is the opposite. The West Indian or Asian does not, by being born in England, become an Englishman. In law he becomes a United Kingdom citizen by birth: in fact, he is a West Indian or an Asian still. Unless he be one of a small minority - for number, I repeat again and again, is of the essence - he will by the very nature of things have lost one country without gaining another, lost one nationality without acquiring a new one (Smithies and Fiddick, 1969;77).

The real problem, he claimed in the Walsall speech, was not discrimination but the migrants' communalism (Smithies and Fiddick, 1969; 22). Powell believed that this was a disintegrative force because it meant the creation of a distinct culture and set of interests which, so he claimed, could be defenced by the legal 'privileges' created by the Race Relations legislation. The explicit, primary object of Powell's concern was, therefore, not the 'race' of the migrants, but with maintaining the cultural homogeneity of the English 'nation'.

Nevertheless, a number of devices were employed in the speeches to sustain the categorisation that the problems arising from 'immigration' were closely connected with the phenotypical difference of the migrant population. First, there were a limited number of strategic references to skin colour. Powell referred to 'white children' or 'white inhabitants', the former being used dramatically in the very first paragraph of the speech given on 9

February, whose lives were alleged to have been made more difficult by 'immigration' (Smithies and Fiddick, 1969:19, 65, 66). Although he was careful to refer to 'immigrants' without specifying any further distinction other than that they were from the Commonwealth, he did make a reference to 'coloured immigrants and their offspring' in the Eastbourne speech (Smithies and Fiddick, 1969:70). Second, in two of the speeches there were references to a supposed danger of reproducing in England a problem that was well-known in the USA. Immediately after claiming that a child born in England of West Indian or Asian parents could not be English, Powell predicted that

> With the lapse of a generation or so we shall at least have succeeded - to the benefit of nobody - in reproducing in 'England's green and pleasant land' the haunting tragedy of the United States (Smithies and Fiddick, 1969:77; cf. pp.21, 73.)

Third, Powell specified precisely the object of his attack by quoting passages from letters he announced he had been sent or by citing conversations with constituents. The most explicit reference came in the speech given on 20 April, 1968, when he claimed that a constituent had told him that

> In this country in fifteen or twenty years time the black man will have the whip-hand over the white man (Smithies and Fiddick, 1969:36).

Powell also cited letters which referred to 'Negroes', to 'coloured' and to West Indian people and which also attributed negative characteristics to the people so categorised (cf. Smithies and Fiddick, 1969:66-8).

The first device utilised an explicit reference to phenotypical difference while the other two worked in somewhat different ways. References to the USA depend on commonsense understandings of the political conflicts that took place in US cities in the 1960s which were widely interpreted, especially in the media, as evidence for the existence of a 'race' problem (Hartman & Husband, 1974:135). Thus, two days after Powell's speech of 9 February 1968, the *Times* had a front page headline 'City Blamed for Race Riot' leading a story about the publication of a report on a riot in the United States in July 1967 (*Times,* 11.2.68). Given that Powell continually emphasised the care with which his speeches were worded, there is considerable significance in the fact that his emphasis upon the category of 'nation' to signify a problem in England was here underpinned by a reference to a situation widely interpreted as having a 'race' problem. The third device operated by legitimating commonsense interpretations of the 'ordinary citizen'. The few references to constituents' statements of despair and alleged victimisation echoed the commonsense imagery of 'race' employed in workplaces, pubs and bus queues about the consequences of the presence of Asian and Caribbean migrants and their children (cf. Phizacklea & Miles, 1980:167-76). All three of these devices therefore substituted for the use of the idea of 'race'.

But it is not so much that Powell's 1968 speeches operated with a sanitised code (Reeves, 1984:189-97) whereby what he 'really meant' was partially obscured by more 'polite' language. Rather, Powell was articulating a theory of nationalism and only by understanding this can we appreciate both the continuity in Powell's ideology (cf. Wood, 1965:135-46) and the nature of the racism that he was articulating (cf. Barker, 1981:42; also Nairn, 1981:256-90). Powell was positing the existence of an enduring politico-cultural unit, the English nation, which is alleged to have a number of equally enduring social and cultural characteristics as well as certain psychological features, for example, a 'strange passivity in the face of danger or absurdity or provocation' (Smithies and Fiddick, 1969:77). The ability of the English 'nation' to survive was said to depend upon protection from, inter alia, sources of internal dissolution and Powell identified the scale of the migrant presence as the source of such dissolution. The migrant population was attributed with the characteristics of not only intensifying the struggle for scarce resources (e.g. taking the hospital beds tha should rightfully be occupied by English mothers) but also with threatening the foundation of continued existence of the English nation. The 'alien wedge' was the 'enemy within'.

Not only was this 'internal enemy' surreptitiously identified by phenotypical features. In a crucial passage Powell claimed that the process of disintegration was taking place not only by means of cultural differentiation but also through 'race':

> Now we are seeing the growth of positive forces acting against integration, of vested interests in the preservation and sharpening of racial and religious differences, with a view to the exercise of actual domination, first over fellow-immigrants and then over the rest of the population (Smithies and Fiddick, 1969:42).

Powell here warned that a difference of 'race', hand in hand with cultural variation, and manipulated by forces within the migrant population, threatened the survival of the English 'nation'. Powell's theory of nationalism therefore contained the idea of 'race' at its centre. This, in turn, is consistent with his references to the United States and thus, in the paragraph that follows the one cited above, Powell predicts

> That tragic and intractable phenomenon which we watch with horror on the other side of the Atlantic but which there is interwoven with the history of the States itself, is coming upon us here by our own volition and our own neglect (Smithies and Fiddick, 1969:43).

The primary emphasis upon 'nation' was closely linked to the solution to the problem he identified. Although he reiterated the demand for further restrictions on entry into England (cf. Smithies and Fiddick, 1969:37), his main concern was to refocus the political debate, away from 'immigration' and onto the natural reproduction of the migrant population within England. He defined this fact as the major problem then and for the future:

> As time goes on, the proportion of this total who are immigrant descendants, those born in England, who arrived here by exactly the same route as the rest of us, will rapidly increase. Already by 1985 the native-born would constitute the majority. It is this fact above all which creates the extreme urgency of action now, of just that kind of action which is hardest for politicians to take, action where the difficulties lie in the present but the evils to be prevented or minimised lie several parliaments ahead (Smithies and Fiddick, 1969:36-7; 70-4).

Consequently, 'strict immigration control', although necessary, was insufficient, and an active policy of 'repatriation' was necessary to avert the 'impending disaster' (Smithies and Fiddick, 1969:74). Powell believed that this policy required the formation of a Ministry of Repatriation to organise the necessary 're-emigration', and his defence of the English 'nation' required the physical removal of the 'alien presence'.

The ultimate justification for this was not that the English population would not endure the process which 'dislodged' them from 'their country and ... their home towns' (Smithies and Fiddick, 1969:73), but that such endurance was impossible because of 'human nature':

> I do not believe it is in human nature that a country, and a country such as ours, should passively watch the transformation of whole areas which lie at the heart of it into alien territory (Smithies and Fiddick, 1969:74).

The political task, then, was to bring policy into line with 'human nature'. So, in the 1968 speeches, there was a logical link between the idea of 'nation' and the policy of 'repatriation', and the primary emphasis placed on these two categories can be interpreted as the construction and assertion of a new dualism, that of 'nation/ repatriation'. The dualism was underpinned by a reference to a hypothetical 'human nature'.

Powell's 1968 speeches, and the 'nation/ repatriation' categorisation that they promulgated were a challenge to Labour government policy articulated in its 1965 White Paper, and subsequently developed in its attempt to legislate for 'race relations' by making racial discrimination illegal. That challenge developed from an agreement that 'immigration' was a legitimate object of political attention, that it caused problems (e.g. both claimed that it led to increased pressure on hospital facilities) and that it should therefore be strictly limited. The challenge exposed the emergent contradiction in the Labour Government's interpretation insofar as it was attempting to shift the focus of political attention away from the migrant population and towards the reaction to it (i.e. discrimination and its effects), but only after it had firmly categorised the migrant presence as problematic by endorsing the 'race/ immigration' dualism, and by reinforcing discrimination at the point of entry into Britain.

Powell exposed this contradiction by seizing the Labour Government's 1965 category of 'integration' and typifying the migrant population as the main threat to its achievement. This he did, not with the idea of 'race', but with the idea of 'nation', conceived as a homogeneous cultural unit with a distinctive history (cf. Wood, 1965:144-6). Powell's argument was that the coherence of the 'nation' was subverted by the presence of a migrant group which was consciously reproducing its distinctiveness of 'race' and culture. Consequently, the 'English people' were the real victims of 'immigration' and this inferior position, so the argument continued, was reinforced by the attempt to legislate on behalf of 'race relations'. Powell insisted logically that the 'alien wedge' had to be 'repatriated' if the historical and cultural unity of the 'English people' was to be maintained. Powell's 'nation/ repatriation' dualism, however, carefully subsumed and legitimated the 'race/ repatriation' dualism by implicitly and explicitly claiming that the threat to the unity of the 'nation' came from the reproduction of differences of 'race' and culture, as well as the appropriation of services designed for 'our people'.

The validity and significance of this argument can be illustrated by considering some aspects of the political and ideological context of and reaction to Powell's intervention which I illustrate from reporting in the *Times*.

First, it needs to be emphasised that Powell's speeches were condemned and his sacking from the Shadow Cabinet was supported by leading articles. On 22 April 1968, the *Times* ran a leading article titled 'An Evil Speech' in which his Birmingham speech was defined as 'racialist', while the leading article in the *Times* on 18 November 1968, following the Eastbourne speech, was headed 'A Doctrine of Fear' and included this assertion:

> When one reads Mr. Powell's speech, right through, in this light one is bound to conclude that he is hostile to coloured people in Britain, that he is afraid of them, and that they have reason to be afraid of him.

However, and second, these leading articles found little reason to disagree with the policies that he advocated, nor with the general framework of his analysis. The concern expressed was not about the suggestion that 'repatriation' was the key to solving the problems created by migration but, as it was argued in the *Times* leader on 22 April 1968, about the fact that Powell did not discuss the problems in 'reasonable terms'.

Third, and most significantly in this context, much of the reporting employed the 'race/ immigration' dualism. This is evident in the quotation cited above. In addition, on the 10 February 1968, the *Times* had reported:

> By the end of the century Britain would have a racial problem as big as that of the United States unless immigration policy was changed, Mr. Enoch Powell, Conservative front bench spokesman on defence, said at a Conservative dinner in Walsall last night.

This picked up Powell's unspecific reference to the problem in the United States and explicitly labelled it as a problem of 'race'. This was repeated and reinforced by a lengthy analysis in the *Times* on 22 April 1968 titled 'What Britain can Learn from America' in which it was argued that legislating to make racial discrimination illegal was not a 'cure-all for the race problem'. Again, on the 23 April 1968, the leader of the Opposition, Mr. Heath, was described as holding the view that:

> The law was only part of the solution to the race problem. Experience in North America showed it was only a limited part.

The transposition also occurred although not systematically, in the *Times* headlines:
'Appeal for Restraint on Race' (23 April 1968): 'Widespread Split over Powell's Race Speech' (25 April 1968): and 'Mounting Volume of Race Protest' (25 April 1968).

Finally, there was an explicit repetition of the 'race/ immigration' dualism in a *Times* leading article titled 'Incomers from Kenya' on 13 February 1968 in which it was argued that

> ... any large influx of coloured immigrants to Britain at this time is likely to put an added strain on race relations in this country ... The great danger for Britain is of a depressed coloured proletariat, where the problems of race and of poverty are synonymous.

Of equal significance is the political and ideological interaction between Powell and the British population. One insight into this interaction can be found from the large number of people who wrote to him following his speeches. Spearman analysed a sample of some 100,000 letters that Powell received following the Birmingham speech of 20 April 1968, which demonstrates the interaction between the ideas of 'race' and 'nation' in commonsense. Of those letters supporting Powell, a sample of 3437 were analysed to identify the reasons given. Only a small minority (71) were classified as articulating racism while approximately one third (1128) were classified as claiming that immigration was threatening British culture and traditions. Some of the extracts cited in the report echo this interconnection of 'race' and 'nation':

> I want above all else an integrated society and I am convinced this can never come about if a large racial minority is allowed to build up. In my work as a town planner I come across the problems posed by too hasty immigration.

> No reasonable man would hate another just because he has a darker skin, but it would be blind to pretend that coloured immigration on the scale we now see does not endanger the Englishness of England. It is not ignoble to wish one's children and grandchildren to grow up in the English traditions and way of life which our forebears fostered. Nor is it ignoble that we should wish to avoid the danger that these traditions and beliefs would be distorted by too many of alien origins and 'ethos' (Spearman, 1968:668).

More generally, Spearman's analysis demonstrates the widespread categorisation of the migrants in the letters by reference to phenotypical characteristics and of the migrant presence as creating problems for the English population:

> The words foreign or black or coloured invasion are freely used. A sense of being overwhelmed by an unforeseen, unplanned event is expressed ... The letters reflect the feeling that *they* by their actions have produced problems for *us,* which do not in any way affect *them* and which they are not doing anything to help us solve. *Their* idea is to tell *us* what we must and must not do (1968:669).

There is some evidence to support the contention that Powell was successful in shifting the 'race/ immigration' dualism articulated by a large proportion of the English population to incorporate the 'repatriation' theme. First, and here opinion poll data is uncritically accepted, in April 1968, 64% of a sample agreed that 'coloured immigrants who are already here should be encouraged to go home' (Studlar, 1974:377). There was, therefore, majority support for what was assumed to be Powell's demand. However, and secondly, there is significance in the fact that the question was asked at all. Studlar notes that the first time such a question was asked was in March 1968 and goes on to imply that because this preceded the April 1968 speech, Powell is shown again to have been following public opinion, although he also notes that the proportion supporting such a policy increased after the Birmingham speech (1974:375-6). This is misleading, if not incorrect. Powell made an explicit reference to the policy role of 'voluntary repatriation' in the Walsall speech in February 1968 (Smithies and Fiddick, 1969:20) and the NOP organisation asked a 'repatriation' question in March 1968. Opinion poll organisations are themselves part of the political and ideological process, and not neutral observers, because they are engaged in the selection of topics and questions as indicators of public opinion, and this is a necessarily selective process. This is revealed by a decision to ask a new question as this means an addition to the stock of issues considered to constitute 'public opinion'. As Edelman argues:

> To define beliefs as public opinion is itself a way of creating opinion, for such a reference both defines the norm that should be democratically supported and reassures anxious people that authorities respond to popular views (1977:49-50).

The decision to ask a 'repatriation' question was a legitimation of Powell's analysis and an indication of his success in redefining the political agenda.

But Powell's 'nation/ repatriation dualism only overlaid and did not replace the already established 'race/ immigration' dualism. This is evident in the discrepancy between the various questions asked by the opinion poll organisations and the precise terms of the policy that Powell advocated. Powell demanded the 'repatriation' only of 'immigrants', a term that was occasionally made more specific by the adjective 'Commonwealth'. In March, May and December 1968, the opinion poll question was; 'Do you think the immigrants already in Britain should be encouraged by government grants to return home?' In June 1969, the question was; 'Mr. Powell has suggested that grants be made available to help coloured immigrant families go back to their countries of origin. Do you agree or disagree with this suggestion?', a formulation that does not accord with the precise wording of Powell's 1968 speeches. These discrepancies are a measure of the way in which the 'race/ immigration' dualism filtered the 'nation/ repatriation' dualism and are therefore a measure of its predominance as commonsense; 'immigrants' was an established ideological category which referred to those of different 'race', and hence they were liable to 'repatriation'. Powell's contribution was to offer the category of 'nation' to justify such a policy, but this primary category subsumed the idea of 'race'.

Conclusion
Powell's political intervention in 1968 occurred at a critical conjuncture. The Labour Government, although ideologically trapped by the 'race/ immigration' dualism, was partially attempting to transcend it by strengthening the law which made racial discrimination illegal. This initiative meant shifting the focus of political attention away from the 'immigrants' and onto the reaction within England to their presence and its implications for their quality of life. Although the necessary legislation was passed, Powell gained the political initiative and ensured that the 'immigrant' presence and its supposed effects remained the primary object of attention. This was

achieved not only by means of what he said but also by the political and media reaction to what he said. The resulting intensification of the racialisation of domestic English politics was maintained by a series of speeches in which the category of 'nation' predominated but in which there were allusions to the phenotypical characteristics of the migrants. These allusions drew upon and were sustained by a widespread, commonsense acceptance of 'race' as a biological reality and by the media's use of the 'race' category. These were moments in an ideological process that sustained the fiction that 'race' was a reality which needed to be legislated for. But in the light of this, how are we to categorise the content of Powell's speeches?

I have emphasised throughout that Powell did not systematically employ the idea of 'race', nor did he assert that the migrants were biologically inferior. The content of these speeches does not accord therefore with the main features of the scientific racism of the nineteenth century. Indeed, the primary object was not the migrants but the English 'nation' or 'way of life'. Powell's central assertion was that the continued existence of this 'nation' was threatened by the presence of an 'immigrant' population which he emphasised as being both culturally and phenotypically distinct. He further predicted that the consequence of this presence would be an American-style tragedy, his most powerful allusion to the idea of 'race'.

I have argued elsewhere that the defining characteristic of racism as ideology

> ... ascribes negatively evaluated characteristics in a deterministic manner (which may or may not be justified) to a group which is additionally identified as being in some way (phenotypically or genotypically) distinct (Miles, 1982:78).

Using this definition, Powell's 1968 speeches warrant description as racism. Indeed, his argument reproduced the main features of the racist theory of history which asserts a natural or biological foundation for conflict between discrete populations characterised by a distinct biology and culture. His intention was to highlight and reinforce a sense of national cohesion or 'imagined community' (Anderson, 1983) by signifying the Asian and West Indian presence as a disintegrative intrusion. This worked not by labelling these migrant populations as inferior 'races' but by signifying the English as a 'nation' whose very existence was threatened by the creation, through immigration and then natural reproduction, of a 'race' problem. It is not necessary to posit a hierarchy of biological superiority/ inferiority to ascribe to a group a cultural and biological homogeneity and capacity to bring about the dissolution of a similarly constituted group. What matters is that the two, or more, groups are reified as natural entities, each with ascribed, unchanging characteristics, and are then said to be naturally incompatible. In this sense, whether the 'race' of the 'nation' category is explicitly applied is of secondary significance for each is capable of working ideologically with the same outcome. In other words, each category can subsume the other.

The racialisation of domestic English politics, and the articulation of racism that sustained that process, were central features shaping the incorporation of migrant workers and their families into English civil society and into the relations of capitalist production. The migration from the Caribbean and the Indian subcontinent had its origin in the uneven development of the capitalist mode of production in what an increasing demand for labour in England in the 1950s articulated with an economically surplus population in colonies and ex-colonies where capitalist development was weak. These migrants were recruited to semi- and unskilled positions in the hierarchy of wage labour, but only because no other labour was available. A study conducted in the early 1960s demonstrated that employers had only engaged 'coloured workers' during the 1950s when all other sources had been exhausted (Wright, 1968:40-7): they were recruiting labour on the basis of a racialised hierarchy of acceptability, as the following illustrates:

> After the war there was firstly a shortage of workers, and secondly, a sense of freedom amongst the workers generated by the attitude of the people coming home from the forces. They felt that because they had fought for freedom, they deserved a job, and could pick and choose, so they didn't like settling down. We tried employing continentals and refugees, etc., but it didn't work out in our industry. The Chairman after the war wouldn't have foreigners (this meant coloured workers). He died in 1949, and in 1950 the succeeding Chairman employed Indian workers (Wright, 1968:42).

It is therefore no surprise that Asian and Carribbean workers were also found to be more likely to be unemployed in periods of unemployment (Wright, 1968:85).

Subsequent studies have confirmed Wright's conclusions and have demonstrated the pervasive influence of discrimination in the recruitment and promotion of such workers (Daniel, 1968; Smith, 1977; Brown, 1984). The implication of these findings is that discriminatory practices ensured that Caribbean and Asian workers were retained in those positions to which they were recruited because no other labour was available. In such circumstances, racism becomes an ideological relation of production because its articulation legitimates the processes which locate and confine agents, categorised using the idea of 'race', to specific positions in the hierarchy of wage labour. In other words, the capital accumulation process leaves certain sites in the production/ circulation process vacant, and racism operates as one of the allocative mechanisms to those positions.

By the late 1960s, the Caribbean and the Indian subcontinent no longer served as a labour reservoir for the capitalist mode of production in England, although a migration of dependents of earlier migrant workers continued. The state was faced with the contradictory effects of the articulation of racism. The labour power of these racialised migrants had been incorporated into key sectors of the economy, and was retained there by discriminatory practice, yet in the course of the racialisation of political relations, racism defined the migrant presence as undesirable. The response of the Labour government to this contradiction was to attempt to eliminate discriminatory practice in order to allow these racialised agents to compete equally for scarce resources (e.g. hospital beds, housing and, by this time, jobs) while simultaneously legitimating the 'race/ immigration' dualism. Such a response reinforced the contradiction. Powell's intervention was ideologically consistent and politically radical. Within civil society, the 'race' problem was to be resolved by repatriating its alleged source, the migrants, but Powell was equally aware of the role of migrant labour in a capitalist economy. Consequently, he argued that

> ... the remedy for shortage of labour in a developed economy is more capital and better organisation (Smithies and Fiddick, 1969:69).

Where conditions ruled out such an increase in constant capital relative to variable capital, another solution was available:

> It need not even follow that the income from work done here in Britain would be suddenly lost to the home communities if permanent settlement of population were replaced by what many countries in Europe and elsewhere are familiar with - the temporary, albeit often long-term, intake of labour (Smithies and Fiddick, 1969:76).

Whether such a solution should have avoided the problem that Powell identified is unlikely, given the consequences of contract labour migration elsewhere in Europe (cf. Castles, et al., 1984). But what is significant here is that Powell's political intervention in 1968 had an ideological consistency in that it identified the migrant presence and the consequences of that presence as problematic and offered a solution which required the removal of that presence. Moreover, by careful allusion, his political intervention was able to utilise the commonsense conception of 'race' in the construction of a radical nationalism which the *Times* of 18 November 1968 labelled 'the new tribalism'. In so doing, Powell played a key role in sustaining the ideological conditions under which the myth of 'race' continued to give meaning to the process by which migrant workers and their families were incorporated into the political and economic relations of English capitalism. The maintenance of that myth obscured the racism that sustained it and the inferior position of the migrants in political and economic relations.

Bibliography

Anderson, B.	(1983)	*Imagined Communities* London, Verso
Banton, M.	(1970)	'The Concept of Racism' in S. Zubaida, (ed.) *Race and Racialism* London, Tavistock
Banton, M.	(1977)	*The Idea of Race* London, Tavistock
Barker, M.	(1981)	*The New Racism* London, Junction Books
Brittan, A. & Maynard, M.	(1984)	*Sexism, Racism and Oppression* Oxford, Basil Blackwell
Brown, C.	(1984)	*Black and White Britain* London, Heinemann
Castles, S. et al.	(1984)	*Here for Good* London, Pluto Press
Daniel, W.W.	(1968)	*Racial Discrimination in England* Harmondsworth, Penguin
Edelman, M.	(1977)	*Political Language: Words That Succeed and Politics That Fail* New York, Academic Press
Gaskell, E.	(1980)	'Managing the "Underclass"; a Further Note on the Sociology of Race Relations in Britain' *Race & Class* 22(1), 47-62
Hartman, P. & Husband, C.	(1974)	*Racism and the Mass Media* London, Davis-Poynter
HMSO	(1965)	*Immigration from the Commonwealth* London, HMSO
Joshi, S. & Carter, B.	(1984)	'The Role of Labour in the Creation of a Racist Britain' *Race and Class* 25(3), 53-70
Joshua, H. et al.	(1983)	*To Ride the Storm* London, Heinemann
Layton-Henry, Z.	(1984)	*The Politics of Race in Britain* London, George Allen & Unwin
MacDougall, H.A.	(1982)	*Racial Myth in English History* Montreal, Harvest House
Miles, R.	(1982)	*Racism and Migrant Labour: A Critical Text* London, Routledge & Kegan Paul
Miles, R.	(1984a)	'Marxism versus the "Sociology of Race Relations"?' *Ethnic & Racial Studies* 7 (2), 217-37
Miles, R.	(1984b)	'The Riots of 1958; the Ideological Construction of "Race Relations" as a Political Issue in Britain' *Immigrants and Minorities,* 3 (3), 252-75
Miles, R. & Phizacklea, A.	(1984)	*White Man's Country: Racism in British Politics* London, Pluto Press
Montagu, A.	(1972)	*Statement on Race* London, Oxford University Press
Nairn, T.	(1981)	*The Break-up of Britain* London, Verso
Phizacklea, A. & Miles, R.	(1980)	*Labour and Racism* London, Routledge & Kegan Paul
Piore, M.J.	(1979)	*Birds of Passage: Migrant Labour and Industrial Societies* Cambridge, Cambridge University

Pitt-Rivers, J.	(1970)	'Race Relations as a Science; A Review of Michael Banton's "Race Relations"' *Race,* 11, 335-42
Reeves, F.	(1984)	*British Racial Discourse* Cambridge, Cambridge University Press
Rex, J.	(1970)	*Race Relations in Sociological Theory* London, Weidenfeld & Nicolson
Richmond, A.H.	(1969)	'Sociology of Migration in Industrial and Post-Industrial Societies', in J.A. Jackson, (ed) *Migration* Cambridge, Cambridge University Press
Rose, S. et al.	(1984)	*Not in Our Genes: Biology, Ideology and Human Nature* Harmondsworth, Penguin
Schoen, D.E.	(1977)	*Enoch Powell and the Powellites* London, Macmillan
Smith, D.	(1977)	*Racial Disadvantage in Britain* Harmondsworth, Penguin
Smithies, B. & Fiddick, P.	(1969)	*Enoch Powell on Immigration* London, Sphere Books
Spearman, D.	(1968)	'Enoch Powell's Postbag' *New Society,* 9 May
Studlar, D.	(1974)	'British Public Opinion, Colour Issues, and Enoch Powell; A Longitudinal Analysis', *British Journal of Political Science* 4, 371-81
Studlar, D.	(1978)	'Policy Voting in Britain; The Colored Immigration Issue in the 1964, 1966 and 1970 General Elections' *American Political Science Review* 72(1), 46-64
Wood, J., ed.	(1965)	*A Nation Not Afraid: The Thinking of Enoch Powell* London, B.T. Batsford
Wright, P.L.	(1968)	*The Coloured Worker in British Industry* London, Oxford University Press

Ethnocentrism, Racism, Genocide...

John Lechte

> There is no experience which is not a way of thinking, and which cannot be analysed from the point of view of the history of thought...
> Michel Foucault.

As introduction, I shall examine some aspects of the background to this paper concerning the transition, as I see it, from ethnocentrism in the eighteenth century to genocide in the twentieth.

When I came to reflect on the cultural construction of race, I posed some fairly obvious questions; How can one understand the concept (or 'idea', as Robert Miles in this volume has argued) of 'race' in the eighteenth century when European voyagers began 'discovering' different societies at an increasingly rapid rate? Is it the same as the term we use today? Or is it that we tend to conflate two things; ethnocentrism, which has been with us for centuries, and today's term 'race'? I came to the view that the least one could do was pay some attention to what has been written about race, how it emerged within twentieth-century context, especially as regards Natural History and the writings of voyagers and naturalists. To begin in this way means that conclusions other than those we are used to have to be entertained. We have to consider, for instance, the possibility that 'race' as it initially appeared in Western thought had nothing to do with the notion of race we understand today, even if many historians fail to recognise this.

Indeed, upon consideration, it seemed reasonably clear to me that what I call eighteenth-century ethnocentrism (exemplified in the thought of the Enlightenment) is certainly not the same thing as nineteenth- or twentieth-century racism. Moreover, I contend that we are all ethnocentric up to a point, but not necessarily racist.

In light of the above remarks, I now outline some of my own thought processes in seeking to clarify the issues involved, and then discuss what I think are some pertinent arguments put forward by Michel Foucault about race and politics in the twentieth century.

I am confining my remarks to a particular kind of discontinuity in European thinking about the 'other', one that is associated both with the change from absolute monarchies to the rise of nation states in Europe and with Europe's developing hegemony over the colonial world. Like Foucault, I see discontinuities in history but to analyse them it is sometimes necessary to write as if history were continuous.

What initially led to my reconsideration of the notion of race was my reading about the ethnocentrism of eighteenth-century voyagers' encounters with, or blindness to, the sacred and the profane in Pacific societies. In this context, I was particularly interested in Mary Douglas's study of the sacred; in *Purity and Danger* (1979) Douglas alludes to the paradox that the sacred is inscribed *in* the profane, a point that has been further exploited by Julia Kristeva in *Powers of Horror* (1982). Both Douglas's and Kristeva's treatment of the sacred, I thought, was bound to expose a European's blindness to the effect of the sacred in an alien culture, if not in their own. And indeed, to some extent I believe that this can be demonstrated. Part of what I have to say below will confirm this point.

When we come to examine the views of the sacred expressed in the accounts of members of Bougainville's voyage in the Pacific, there is no doubt that we are confronted - as one might expect from the disciples of Rousseau - with ethnocentrist views regarding the non-European other's notion of the sacred (cf. Taillemite, 1977). This other, I thought I could show, with its own peculiar version of the sacred, would be a quintessentially *racial* other. With just a slight change of register, I believed, this ethnocentrism could be seen as a form of racism - or at least as 'racentrism' resulting from thought that used race as one if its categories for describing the world.

The Pacific, after all, is well-entrenched in Western mythology. The 'noble' and/ or 'ignoble savage' can easily seem to offer the basis of a racist view of the world (cf. B. Smith, 1969). I began to think that the sacred (let us define it loosely as a series of interdictions, as a system of 'inclusions' and 'exclusions', as well as that which is bound up with the inexpressible origin of society, the individual, of life) was the domain which, most of all, became the vehicle for constituting the other as inferior, that is, racially speaking. What scholars tell us today about the term *tapu* might even be seen to confirm this point.

They argue that the key term *tapu* in Pacific cultures - a term which has to do with rituals relating to the sacred, with what should be done as well as with what should not be done - came to be understood as the exclusively interdictive term of European coinage, 'taboo'. Thus in the Pacific islands of the Marquesas, when the first Europeans arrived, women had to swim out to the ships because the canoes were *tapu*. Similarly, hogs were never traded because they were *tapu*. Again, it was *tapu* for men to be below decks while women were above: *tapu* for men to eat with women or touch their clothing, or their sleeping mats (Dening 1980:51). And if *tapu* was all there was, then, for the eighteenth-century Frenchman especially, this was for the equivalent of there being no religious system at all. Bougainville, for instance, asked while at Tahiti whether the people had a religion. And he answered his own question by saying:

> I have seen no temple, no external manifestation of adoration: such acts of devotion as we have performed before [the Tahitians] have neither struck nor interested them. In the houses of the important people, large wooden figures are to be found, one of each sex. In order to establish whether these were idols, we went on bended knee before them, then spat at their feet, stepped upon them. Each of these very different acts drew the derision of the Indian spectators 15 April 1758ı (Taillemite, 1977:328. My translation).

Not to have tangible and familiar evidence of religion - of the sacred - was reason to doubt its presence. But what if the sacred were tied up with the intangible, the implicit, the inexpressible, the secret? Or what if the very absence of any outward, visible manifestation of the sacred were indeed a kind of negative index of its power? Might it not be, finally, that disguise is one of the sacred's most profound characteristics? Questions of this kind are not new: but they do nevertheless serve to remind us of the ambiguous and shifting boundary that emerges between two cultures and of two quite different modes of thought. We certainly have the basis of ethnocentrism here in European attitudes to the sacred, but do we have the basis of racism as well? This is the issue I elaborate in the following pages. My conclusion will suggest that an initial assumption about continuities between eighteenth and twentieth century thinking need revision. We need to distinguish very clearly between eighteenth century ethnocentrism and twentieth century racism and not conflate the two.

If there is an idea of race in the eighteenth century, it seems to be very different from that of the latter part of the nineteenth and of the twentieth century. Nevertheless, it also seems to be true that many eighteenth-century forms of thought are still with us today. This is particularly so with regard to the law and politics; but, more specifically, what Rousseau says about 'natural' woman is still very influential in many quarters. Indeed, something seems to have occurred at the level of discourse and language - or more precisely, has not occurred - which has led to our commonly-used terminology and modes of expression being out of kilter with the changing circumstances in which we find ourselves.

In this regard, Jacques Attali in his book, *Noise* (1985), makes the point that it is not so much thought as music and its changes which often prefigure and at times accompany social and economic changes. Thus, Attali writes that;

> [Music] heralds, for it is *prophetic*. It has always been in its essence a herald of times to come. Thus ... if it is true that the *political organization of the twentieth century is rooted in the political thought of the nineteenth, the latter is almost entirely present in embryonic form in the music of the eighteenth century* (1985:4, emphasis in original).

If we consider this point, we note that for some reason political discourse today is largely that of the juridical state: our references to sexuality and power are still largely those of the Romantics: our notions of the economy and society remain those of the theorists of wealth and the Social Contract. I am not only referring to the language of everyday life, but also to the language of specialists, and to the growing dominance in the late eighteenth century of representation which made stereotypes possible. With the French Revolution there emerged in Europe a more or less fully developed state apparatus founded on the principle of representation (e.g., 'state' = nation). The eighteenth century also bequeathed a mode of subjectivity which corresponded to the conscious 'self' or psychological subject, that is, an entirely secular subject which began to treat the irrational, the non-conceptual, the unrepresentable, the feminine and 'mystical' dimensions of the individual and the world (the sacred, in a word) with scepticism and disdain.

With regard to race and racism, people still tend to speak as though these were the products of certain arrogant, egocentric nations, groups or individuals who are out to further their own interests against other nations, groups and individuals, largely through the use of force. We still speak, indeed, as though egotistical self-interest (a very eighteenth-century term if ever there was one) is at the heart of what is wrong with the world. This explains to me how (if not why) ethnocentrism and racism have been conflated. It is as though the language-cum-discourse of everyday life in the twentieth century has been bequeathed to us by the late eighteenth and early nineteenth centuries: and this can lead us to reflect upon the notion that even the category 'everyday life' and the attendant opposition of appearance and reality (which so concerned Rousseau and Kant, albeit in different ways) were also bequeathed to us by the neo-Platonism of the late eighteenth century. I say all this simply as a reminder that the language we use needs to be reflected upon at length.

Turning back to the eighteenth century for a moment, I believe the ethnocentrism evident in the observations and interpretations of that time concerning various forms of exotic behaviours and the levels of so-called civilisation attained by very different peoples, was the result of more of a

European cultural blindness than of any desire to rid the world of diversity, or make the human species 'racially' pure. In this sense particularly, eighteenth century ethnocentrism differs profoundly from modern forms of racism.

Consider Buffon's (1749) writings, for example. Here, we find that Bonnet's 'immense variety' (1779a:212) of nature required a long and laborious effort of observation which eventually provided the basis of a system for classifying nature - both the realm of the inanimate and the animate - into a hierarchical table of imperceptible gradations' with God at the head. As Robinet would have it in representing Buffon's position; 'All matter is organic and living ... Inorganic matter, dead and inanimate, is a chimera, an impossibility' (1768:7). In effect, we are yet to arrive at the point where the three domains of 'animal', 'vegetable' and 'mineral' are relatively discontinuous with one another.

Moreover, so-called objective description was the stock-in-trade of the eighteenth-century naturalist. Thus Buffon urges that,

> ... in order to describe exactly, it is necessary to have seen, examined and compared the thing that is being described, and all this without prejudice, without an idea of system; without this, the description no longer has the character of truth which is the only thing it should embody (1749:25).

Such a statement indicates that to describe nature truthfully there should be no rush to judgement, no hasty generalistions based on mere prejudice. In other words, this is hardly the approach of latter-day racism.

Despite all this, it is also true that accounts by eighteenth century voyagers and naturalists of the peoples they saw are locked into another set of exigencies; the need to satisfy a public's voracious appetite for stories of the 'bizarre, the 'pittoresque' and the avowedly 'exotic'. Books by voyagers sold more than any other genre in the latter half of the eighteenth century (Smith 1821:32). Few published accounts of the time are entirely free from the distortions produced by the pressure of this public demand. These distortions were no doubt spurred on by assertions like those of Robinet (1768:168) concerning the existence of 'Negroes with tails', and of course there are the interminable references to the Patagonian giants. Even so reputable a naturalist as Commerson (the French Banks), who sailed with Bougainville into the Pacific, accepted as valid the stories of the giants' existence (Commerson 1766: Fol. 76).

Such distortions could well be called fictions. This designation does not necessarily contradict the notion that everything in nature is somehow connected to everything else, or that nature is a continuous whole of infinite gradations. It is merely to assert that in constructing 'fictions' people were either poor observers, or that the voids in the existing state of knowledge meant that certain phenomena appeared in isolation, and thus in sharp relief, when compared with other phenomena. The task, at least in principle, was to fill these voids, to *name* the visible world in its entirety, to bring it into the Symbolic Order (the realm of consciousness) and thereby place the exotica and the bizarre in perspective, and thus transform them into the 'ordinary'. Bonnet thus asks:

> ... are we to judge the chain of Beings by our existing knowledge? Because we discover here and there in this chain some interruptions, some voids, are we to conclude that these voids are real? ... We can only begin by covering the vast exhibition rooms of nature; and among this innumerable multitude of diverse productions that she has assembled, how many of them are there that we have not even glimpsed and the existence of which we do not suspect? (1781:197)

In effect, knowledge of the 'known' cannot serve as the model for the 'unknown', for the models have been varied to infinity. 'Difference' is not excluded as a matter of course. As a result, every natural historian is at some point likely to resemble

> a French voyager who would expect to find in the *Terres Australes* the manners of his own country, and who would be quite scandalised not to see them there. The animal kingdom, too, has its *Terres Australes,* where it is probably not normal to have a brain, a heart, a stomach, etc. (Bonnet, 1781:182).

In sum, whatever else it is, eighteenth-century natural history is inclusive rather than exclusive. Everything is necessary in the whole that is nature. Ethnocentrism there may be: but it is an ethnocentrism which is profoundly paternalistic in its attitudes to other societies and cultures rather than openly hostile and aggressive - at least initially. It is thought which, at least in principle, strives to comprehend individuality and diversity, not to destroy it through fear and blind prejudice.

The issues raised here do, to be sure, need to be unravelled still further. However, my purpose in drawing attention to them is simply to bring to mind the nature of the dilemma they evoke: the dilemma of how one can ever escape the confines of one's own culture in order to know the culture of the other.

It is this dilemma that Claude Lévi-Strauss refers to in, among other places, his famous essay written for UNESCO in 1952, entitled *Race and History* (1978:323-362). Lévi-Strauss argues that the notion that 'one culture is unable to hold true judgement about another' because it is caught 'in a relativism without appeal' (1978:344) is true only at the level of abstract logic. In fact, he says, if we look around us we will see that no culture is entirely cut off from all others, and it is unlikely that this has ever been the case in human history. Lévi-Strauss thus argues for the interconnectedness of all cultures, with borrowings and contacts of one kind or another always having taken place. Indeed, he suggests that, far from isolation being the catalyst that produces differences, it is more often than not the very proximity of one culture to another which leads, and has led, to energetic assertions of cultural identity (1978:328). For Lévi-Strauss, this means, too, that there has never been a 'pure' race: that there are no 'innate racial aptitudes', as there are no 'aptitudes related to the anatomical or physiological constitution of black, yellow and white races' (1978:325).In short, there is no biological basis for race - something to which I will return.

What does exist is a diversity of societies and civilisations in human history, each of which has been creative and progressive in its own way through having made contacts with other societies and civilisations. This diversity suggests the idea of an underlying *equality* of humanness in principle between societies and cultures.

If we accept two general points emerging from Lévi-Strauss's *Race and History,* namely, that a pure race does not exist and that nearly every society, whether Western or not, has initially tended to characterise outsiders as barbarians and inferiors without necessarily subjugating them, then, we tend to render benign the very real political ends that the term race and the practice of racism have been made to serve if we simply equate racism with ethnocentrism. From this, it can be seen that certain consequences stem from using the *term* race if, in reality, there is no such thing as a pure race. That is, if among all myths the myth of race is the 'most dangerous', as Ashley Montagu (1974) argues, the political consequences of using the term are also dangerous.

The recent debate about sociobiology has seen eminent biologists such as François Jacob reiterate the view that the concept of race has no real scientific validity (1979:16). For Jacob, it is diversity and difference at the individual and social levels which have been the strength of human biological evolution. It is possible and necessary, I believe, to pursue this argument further.

In the light of the work of Michel Foucault, it is possible to contend that the development of Biology in the nineteenth century is the condition of possibility of the political use of the concept, or term, race in the twentieth. In *The Order of Things,* Foucault argues that, as opposed to the classifying of the visible which dominated the eighteenth century's approximation to our social and natural sciences, the nineteenth century saw the emergence, in the work of Cuvier and others, of the concept of 'life'. Unlike the eighteenth century, the realm of the visible in the nineteenth became connected to the invisible, to the 'deeper' cause of life. Thus Foucault writes:

> From Cuvier onward, it is life in its non-perceptible, purely functional aspect that provides the basis of the exterior possibility of a classification... [T]he possibility of classification now arises from the depths of life, from those elements most hidden from view. Before, the living being was a locality of natural classification: now, the fact of being classifiable is a property of the living being (1973:268).

François Jacob confirms this by pointing to the notion of 'organisation' which by the nineteenth century referred to the *hidden* configuration of beings. 'Organisation', according to Jacob, 'provided a hidden foundation for the bare data of description, for the being as a whole and for its functioning' (1974:83).

Through the concept of 'life', then, and the second-order concept of 'organisation', the interiority - the hidden depths - of individuals and societies became an area open to speculation. These speculations were not, by any means, specific to Biology itself, but opened up the discipline to the prospect of political exploitation which had not existed before. Racism became one of these possibilities. 'Life', 'biology', and the 'body' (both individual and body politic) also came to constitute, in all their complexity, the unconscious frames of reference for all knowledge in the *social* sciences. That is to say, that only when 'life' came to occupy the place once occupied by 'nature' could there be discourses about the bases of social life, the 'health' and 'purity' of the social and individual body, as well as discourses about the human species *as* specifically and separately *human,* rather than as a species which, like any other, was part of nature.

If Foucault's thesis in *The Order of Things* sets up the possibility of a link between 'biology', 'life' and 'race', the first volume of his *History of Sexuality* (1979) - and especially its final part ('Right of Death and Power over Life') - is an even more scandalous proposition concerning the idea of race. Before going into more detail about the argument in this text, I offer some remarks regarding the way Foucault's work may be appreciated, particularly in relation to his discussion of sexuality.

As with much of Foucault's work, the volume on sexuality provides a relentless attempt to contest prevailing stereotypes, to undermine received ideas and to challenge unquestioned presuppositions; in other words, Foucault thinks differently from the guardians of conventional wisdom. This is his strength - and maybe his weakness. For Foucault, to think in the prevailing modes is not really thinking at all. It is necessary to take this into account when coming to grips with his thought.

Take the term 'power', for instance. It is very often used to connote force or oppression; people often refer to the possession of power, or its lack; to the maintenance of order; the police; the state; the law - in short, all that is negative, interdictive, and repressive. For Foucault, however, power does not exist in a vacuum; if it is negative, it still moves against *something* - an object: and this 'object' (e.g. the delinquent, or the criminal) is itself constituted by those with power and knowledge to do so. There is, therefore, no object of power separate from the workings of power - power working in conjunction with the knowledge that marks out its object. The appearance of the delinquent in history is thus a *product* of nineteenth-century power configurations.

To elaborate, I turn to sexuality and its history as it is relevant to race. According to Foucault, sexuality has also been constituted as an object of knowledge and hence power. The repression of sexuality, he argues, did not as is often thought reduce people to silence on the topic. In fact, it was necessary to talk about sex at length if it was to be repressed at all. The perversions and pleasures of sex therefore had to be described, specified and rendered quite explicit. Since the eighteenth century, pedagogical institution, for example, rather than impose a silence on the sex of children and adults has

> multiplied the forms of discourse on the subject; it has established various points of implantation for sex; it has coded contents and qualified speakers. Speaking about children's sex, inducing educators, physicians, administrators and parents to speak of it, or speaking to them about it, causing children themselves to talk about it, and enclosing them in a web of discourses which sometimes address them, sometimes speak about them, or impose canonical bits of knowledge on them, or use them as a basis for constructing a science that is beyond their grasp - all this together enables us to link an intensification of the interventions of power to a multiplication of discourse (Foucault, 1979:29-30).

In keeping with this idea of a proliferation of discourses about sex, Foucault goes on to argue that the so-called repression of sex in the nineteenth-century has to be understood as another stereotype of the Public Culture (the domain of representations) which needs to be challenged. For, in fact, the 'repression' of sex was not the result of any 'renunciation of pleasure or a disqualification of the flesh' (122). Rather, the preoccupations of the time had more to do with 'techniques for maximising life' (123), and the concern was more for talking about 'the body, vigor, longevity, progeniture, and descent of the classes that "ruled"' (ibid) thananything else.

Consequently, sex and sexuality in the modern era from the nineteenth-century onwards has to be understood differently from the way we have been used to. Indeed it is the very domain of pleasure itself - sex - which now has to be seen as implicated in the workings of power to the extent that it has become a mechanism (even a strategy) for (re) producing 'good' health and physical perfection at both the individual and social levels.

What Foucault had in mind here were the immense public health improvement programmes in the nineteenth century (slum clearances, sewerage installations and the like) combined, at the private level, with concern for improvements to the genetic stock in the family, in its 'history'. That is, by comparison with the earlier aristocratic concern about nobility ('blood'), the bourgeoisie could pass on 'good' - or perhaps 'bad' - health, depending on whether they were combining 'healthy' or 'degenerate' genetic stock. A bourgeois marriage thus became the 'consummation' of two genetic pools of physical and mental family attributes. The bourgeoisie's 'blood' (nobility) was therefore found in its good health or, in Foucault's words, 'the bourgeoisie's "blood" was its sex'. This sex, it is worth pointing out, is not the sexuality of Freud but the sex of biology, demography and public health, that is, the sex concerned with the 'themes of health, progeny, race, the future of the species, the vitality of the social body...' (Foucault, 1979:147). That is, it is the sexuality which constitues 'techniques for maximising' life.

It is in the context of this great concern, developed during the nineteenth century, for maximising the 'life' of a population that the conditions of the possibility for a virulent racism emerge. In their most extreme formulations, racist arguments attest that there must be no mixing through sex of (biologically) 'inferior' and (biologically) 'superior' peoples. Such mixing places the healthy genetic pool at risk. In the second half of the nineteenth century, Foucault argues,

> Racism took shape ... (racism in its modern, 'biologising', statist form); it was then that a whole politics of settlement (*peuplement*), family, marriage, education, social hierarchisation, and property, accompanied by a long series of permanent interventions at the level of the body, conduct, health, and everyday life, received their colour and their justification from the mythical concern with protecting the purity of blood and ensuring the triumph of the race (1979:149).

Historians have made us aware for some time now that during the nineteenth century, and even more so in the twentieth, public health improved and various diseases were eliminated. It is also generally accepted that the social sciences built up profiles of 'populations' based on a ceaseless monitoring made possible by the collection of statistical data of all kinds; data on health, education, employment and income, sexual practices and fertility, family situation, patterns of consumption, criminality, ethnicity, etc. These statistics provide information which makes it possible to con-

41

struct the 'normal' case, namely, that which is invoked when a picture of society, or a representation of its 'normal' patterns of behaviour, is required. It is a monitoring which Foucault says is an integral part of 'bio-power' - the power relating to the *management* of populations. Because 'normal' behaviour does not exist outside the definition or construction of it, the norm in fact also produces - definitionally - a panoply of perversions which must be specified, studied and observed in their functioning *in order that* they may be controlled, ordered, repressed or even eliminated. There is therefore no perversion without the 'normal' case: no power without knowledge, as there is no power configuration, in Foucault's view, without results of all kinds being produced, i.e. deviations, perversions, abnormalities.

Thus, for Foucault, power and knowledge co-mingle with each other in the late nineteenth and twentieth centuries in a way that is very different from that of the eighteenth. In the latter century, the juridico-discursive' articulation of power had the wherewithal to 'put to death' or to 'let live' when the monarch was thought to be under threat. The monarch, of course could take an individual's life under the guise of protecting himself. In that century, it was the protection of a centre of power - or of force - itself which was at stake, not the control or the management of a population: power therefore was not inscribed in a whole network of social behaviours. Thus the eighteenth century produced society in which sovereignty was symbolised by the sword and where 'blood' was the symbol of nobility - regardless of the mental or physical health of the population or of individuals. Wars were fought between the troops of the sovereign and those of the enemy. Men fought and died in the name of the sovereign: the sovereign had the power to let live or to put people to death. In this kind of society, Kant's extremely revealing statement about the glory and honour of war (in, let us note, *The Critique of Judgement*) makes very pertinent sense:

> War itself, provided it is conducted with order and a sacred respect for the rights of civilians, has something sublime about it, and gives nations that carry it on in such a manner a stamp of mind only the more sublime the more numerous the dangers to which they are exposed, and which they are able to meet with fortitude (1973, Pt. 1: 112—113)

What we need to note, then, is that power in its twentieth century form can no longer be understood as being exclusively interdictory, or, as Kant would have it perhaps, as preserving the life of the sovereign and therefore the nation. Rather, power can now be seen to permeate all those practices which ostensibly preserve the life of a population against the threat of degeneration, and it is this which opens the way to racism in general and to Nazi eugenics in particular. As Montagu points out, the eugenists stand for the view that '"race mixture" should be prevented if "racial" degeneration ... is not to ensue' (1974:329). What is scandalous and no doubt difficult to accept, is that it is also the innocent concerns with well-being, with a healthy sexuality, with life which became the basis of that which is anathema to life; the idea of race. A population became a race, and it is this factor which has potentially enormous consequences for us in the so-called post-modern age. The very existence of the species is indeed at stake.

It is only necessary to recognise the incredible (by nineteenth century standards) development and elaboration of the state and its attendant Public Culture (illustrated in part by the 'monitoring' I mentioned earlier) in the twentieth century, to understand that the very notion of a private sphere that is not itself defined by, and is therefore part of, the Public Culture, is extremely doubtful. Indeed, the social sciences have contributed towards making the most intimate social practices and individual behaviour *public* knowledge. Today, the representation of the nation is in its Public Culture (cf. Horne 1986). We can be sure, too, that, if another world war broke out, it would indeed be between state apparatuses that have become inseparable from the populations which are now also inseparable from the Public Culture. We know that the next world war will be explicitly between populations rather than armies. The seeds for this were sown during the last world war in the bombings of Dresden, London, Hiroshima and Nagasaki - bombings which targetted civilians. Kant could not have understood this: he could not have understood that wars today are no longer between soldiers but include the civilian population. He could not have understood either that a world war today risks genocide on a massive scale, both because the weaponry is nuclear and because the targets would be populations. Nuclear warfare signals the end of the 'military' target. Now, population is pitted against population, 'race' is pitted against 'race'. The almost unimaginable but potential holocausts within and between populations should serve as a terrible warning of what is in store in a nuclear war. Yet, in principle at least, Foucault suggests that genocide has become the 'dream' of modern power - the absolute domination of one population over all the rest - assuming they still existed. As he puts it:

> Wars are no longer waged in the name of a sovereign who must be defended: they are waged on behalf of the existence of everyone: entire populations are mobilised for the purpose of wholesale slaughter in the name of life necessity; massacres have become vital. It is as managers of life and survival, of bodies and the race, that so many régimes have been able to wage so many wars, causing so many men to be killed (1979:137).

In relation to the management of life, war becomes an issue of technology: it no longer has anything whatever to do with courage, honour or, indeed, manliness. A war of races is beyond morality. In terms of Kristeva's *Powers of Horror,* this nuclear, genocidal war is abject, that is, it is not even immoral but entirely a-moral (unimaginable).

The preoccupation with 'race' in our modernity, then, ushers in the possibility of race, nuclear war and genocide becoming inseparable from one another. We are now a long way indeed from the 'ethnocentrism' with which I began this paper.

To sum up, I believe that the usefulness of Foucault's thesis is that we are provided with concepts and a framework that begin to make sense of this *fin de siècle* reality with which we are faced, as far as government and 'race' are concerned. While I also believe that the notion that sex alone is at the heart of the 'norm' is questionable (for has Foucault himself not made sex everything here?), it seems clear that the Enlightenment and its thinking can no longer provide us with a framework capable of understanding the kind of political and social reality we now inhabit. It is necessary to leave the thought of the past if we are going to live in the future.

Furthermore, Foucault indicates that it is necessary to be less naive about the monitoring of populations. For while it may be innocent in intent, it must be recognised that power is inseparable from knowledge; knowledge - especially in the social sciences - is the condition of possibility for the workings of power in the modern era. It is not that knowledge as such is culpable, but that it is dangerous.

To conclude, I would like to say that there is a difference between the past and our modernity on the issue of race, and that Foucault alerts us to something fundamental regarding our situation when he links holocaust, race and nuclear madness together. He connects them in a way that would have been unthinkable less than two centuries ago (and maybe even in 1914) when wars were still fought between armies; when only the guilty were supposed to be punished, when only soldiers were supposed to die in war, and when the power of the king was so specific in its application.

References

1. Attali, Jacques. (1985) *Noise: The Political Economy of Music* Minneapolis, University of Minnesota Press
2. Bonnet, Charles. (1779a) 'Corps organisés' *OEUVRES,* Vol. VI, Neuchâtel
3. Bonnet, Charles. (1779b) 'Mémoires d'histoire naturelle' *OEUVRES,* Vol. ·III, Neuchâtel
4. Bonnet, Charles. (1781) 'Contemplation de la nature' *OEUVRES,* Vol. VIII, Neuchâtel
5. Buffon, Georges Louis Le Clerc. (1749) *Histoire naturelle, généerale et particulière* (14 volumes), Vol. I, Paris
6. Commerson, Philiberti. (1776) 'Sommaire d'observations d'histoire naturelle...' MSS 660, Fol. 76, Biblothèque de l'Arsenal, Paris
7. Dening, Greg. (1980) *Islands and Beaches: Discourse on a Silent Land, Marquesas 1774-1880* Melbourne University Press
8. Douglas, Mary. (1979) *Purity and Danger: An Analysis of the Concepts of Pollution and Taboo* London, Routledge & Kegan Paul
9. Foucault, Michel. (1973) *The Order of Things: An Archaeology of the Human Sciences* New York, Vintage Books
10. Foucault, Michel. (1978) *The History of Sexuality* Vol. I (An Introduction) London, Allen Lane
11. Jacob, François. (1974) *The Logic of Living Systems* London, Allen Lane
12. Jacob, François. (1979, 17 November) 'Science de la vie et planification social' *Le Monde,* Paris
13. Kant, Immanuel. (1973) *The Critique of Judgement,* Part I, (The Critique of Aesthetic Judgement) Oxford University Press
14. Kristeva, Julia. (1982) *Powers of Horror: An Essay on Abjection* New York, Columbia University Press
15. Lévi-Strauss, Claude. (1978) 'Race and History' in *Structural Anthropology* Vol. 2, Harmondsworth, Penguin
16. Lovejoy, Arthur O. (1978) *The Great Chain of Being: A Study in the History of an Idea,* Harvard University Press
17. Montagu, Ashley. (1974) *Man's Most Dangerous Myth: The Fallacy of Race* New York, O.U.P.
18. Robinet, J.B. (1768) *Considérations philosophiques de la gradation naturelle des forms de l'être* Paris, Charles Saillant
19. Smith, Bernard. (1969) *European Vision and the South Pacific, 1768-1850* London, Oxford, and New York, O.U.P.
20. Smith, Sir James Edward (ed.). (1821) *A Selection of the Correspondence of Linnaeus and Other Naturalists* London, Longman
21. Taillemite, E. (ed.) (1977) *Bougainville et ses compagnons autour du monde, 1766-1769* Vol. I, Paris, Imprimerie Nationale.

Australian Governments and the Concept of Race: An Historical Perspective

Andrew Markus

This article examines the development of racial concepts in Australia during the nearly 200 years of European occupation as evident in government action, particularly legislation and statistical categorisation. Attention is confined to a relatively limited body of evidence to facilitate comparability over time. The objective is to distinguish broad patterns, a task which is made difficult by the divided legislative authority within the country.

Confining attention to a limited body of evidence does not, however, dispense with the problem of defining precisely the field of study: how is it to be established that certain actions are based on a 'racial' consciousness while others are not? It is insufficient to rely on a narrow definition to distinguish racial consciousness or perception, for the precise form of concepts, categories and terminology can change over time while basic perspectives remain constant. Thus in a period when racial concepts are undeveloped there may be difficulty in establishing a clear and consistent set of categories; at another time concepts may be fully developed, but categorisation may be hidden for political reasons by, for example, an education test. It is necessary to employ a definition which captures the meaning at the core of racial conceptualisation, and which is sufficiently broad to allow for change over time. The definition adopted below incorporates two elements, the first of which is sufficient to establish a racial consciousness. It entails: (1) perception of physically distinguishable human populations (as distinct from sub-populations, such as divisions based on gender), whose behavioural traits and capacities are seen to be immutable, normally although not necessarily explained in terms of the group's biological characteristics or genetic inheritance; and (2) a belief that as a consequence of the group's immutable characteristics it is inappropriate for its members to be treated on a basis of equality with other members of society. There are therefore two elements to the definition, one concerned with perception and categorisation of human populations, the other with the ensuing consequences. The two elements may, but do not necessarily, co-exist.

It is the argument of this paper that racial consciousness in Australia has passed through four phases; (i) the year to 1850, during which a major concern of governments was Aboriginal dispossession: (ii) the second half of the nineteenth century, which saw the beginning of large scale non-European immigration and the first attempts to develop a unified policy to deal with detribalised Aborigines: (iii) the flowering of racial consciousness from 1890-1940: and (iv) the gradual erosion of this outlook over the last forty years.

The Process of Dispossession - 1850

A first phase may be approximately dated from the beginning of European occupation to the gold rushes of the 1850s. In this period there was minimal immigration of non-Europeans but relations with Aborigines, concerned primarily with the process of dispossession, were of major importance. This periodisation is only a rough approximation, having particular relevance to the southern parts of the continent, for the need to dispossess Aborigines remained the dominating characteristic of relations in many other parts of the continent after 1850, for example, in Queensland as I indicate below.

When dispossession was the major concern of governments, relations were essentially of an immediate and practical nature. The subservient position of Aborigines was not spelled out in legislation but established in practice. There was little perceived need to establish the right to dispossess through legislation, for dispossession rested on a claim that Australia could be treated by the Crown as vacant land. Aborigines were, in theory, British subjects; in resisting the spread of Europeans they were the ones breaking the law, and could be dealt with according to its dictates. In reality there was little regard for the letter of the law, but the point remains that dispossession was effectively achieved under the guise of the existing legal system (Rowley 1970; Frost, 1981; Broome, 1982). The clearest illustration is provided by the activities of the Queensland Native Mounted Police in the second half of the nineteenth century. Although Aborigines retained their notional citizenship the native police treated them as a hostile enemy, beyond the jurisdiction of the British legal system. Queensland governments failed to sanction legislatively this para-military force, deciding instead to hide its activities under a veil of silence (Reynolds 1972:16-20; Evans 1975:55-66). In this context governments had little need for (and hence there was little development of) explicit 'racial' categories in legislation.

The withdrawal of notional citizenship was a slow development. Early forms of discrimination in the legal system were not formally couched in racial terms; Aboriginal evidence, for example, was inadmissable not because of a ban on members of a racial group, but because Aborigines could not take an oath on the Bible. In 1844 South Australia legislated to

47

admit evidence taken without a Bible oath when supported by corroborative evidence, but a similar bill was defeated in New South Wales in 1844 and again in 1849 (Reece 1974:180-2).

Although it is argued that government action was not *formally* grounded in racial consciousness, to all intents and purposes it can be equated with action stemming from such a perspective. Further, racist discourse was developed within sections of the government and the wider community. The major qualification is that within government some held to the view that Aborigines could be absorbed into European society; belief in immutable racial characteristics was sometimes questioned.

1850-1890

A second phase can be approximately dated from 1850 to 1890. Within this period governments were having to meet a changing set of circumstances. First, especially in the south-east of the continent, they were increasingly dealing with Aborigines who survived the process of dispossession. Second, for the first time they encountered large scale immigration of non-Europeans, raising the issue of selective immigration controls and discrimination against certain groups resident in the colonies. These changing circumstances within Australia coincided with the development and refinement of racial thought in the western world generally.

Relations with the surviving Aboriginal populations were characterised by a gradual move to curtail their notional rights and privileges. Early examples of such legislation are to be found in New South Wales; for example, there were attempts to forbid the possession of firearms, a prohibition on the freedom to consume alcohol and, under the vagrancy laws, it was made a crime for Europeans to lodge and wander in company with Aborigines (Reece 1974:188; 15 Vict., No. 4).

Legislators recognised the necessity to define an 'Aborigine', but there was as yet relatively little attention to the definition; in particular, the position of people of mixed descent, to be a significant issue in the twentieth century, received little systematic thought before the 1870s, and there was no attempt to define solely on the basis of supposed biological characteristics. Thus a New South Wales Bill of 1839 defined a 'Half-caste Native' as a person 'brought up and abiding with any tribe of Aboriginal Natives of the said Colony' (3 Vict., No. 16, s.1). Major Victorian legislation of 1869, namely the Act to Provide for the Protection and Management of the Aboriginal Natives, adopted similar wording;

> Every Aboriginal native of Australia and every Aboriginal half-caste or child of a half-caste, such half-caste or child habitually associating and

living with Aboriginals, shall be deemed to be an Aboriginal... (33 Vict., No. 349, s.8).

This Act marked an important transition from isolated enactments which deprived Aborigines of specific rights, to comprehensive legislation which, as well as depriving Aborigines of rights, empowered governments to exercise specific controls. It established the pattern for legislation adopted in other parts of the country in the 1890s and 1900s, and provided the legislative basis to limit the freedom of movement of Aborigines and to control aspects of their lives. It provided the following regulations: (i) for prescribing the place where any Aboriginal or any tribe of Aborigines shall reside; (ii) for prescribing the terms on which contracts for and on behalf of Aboriginals may be made with Europeans; (iii) for apportioning amongst Aboriginals the earnings of Aboriginals under any contract: and (v) for the care, custody and education of the children of Aborigines (33 Vict., No. 349, s.2). It was a feature of legislation dealing with Aborigines that much broader powers were assumed than were actually exercised in the majority of cases: administrators had considerable discretion in deciding, for example, which persons were to be moved to reserves. Among other limitations, governments were unwilling to allocate sufficient resources for full implementation of the legislation. But the 1869 Act was significant in providing the pattern for a new form of relationship.

Within this period legislation also affected a second group of non-Europeans, the Chinese immigrants who attempted to enter the Australian colonies during and after the first gold-rushes of the ¢850s. There were two major types of measures enacted. The primary objective was to limit, for the first time, the entry of a specific category of immigrant. A secondary feature was the abridgement of the rights of members of this category who were already within the colonies; thus, for example, legislation passed in Victoria (1855), New South Wales (1861) and Queensland (1877) restricted the freedom of Chinese to mine on certain goldfields (Price 1974; Markus 1979).

While a precedent was established in limiting entry into the colonies, legislation in most colonies was directed at a narrowly defined group and it was not totally prohibitive: it did not bar the permanent entry of all members of the designated population. The objective of legislation was to limit entry, and to do so more severely with the passage of time, but not to impose a total ban in the period to 1890. Thus in 1855 Victoria imposed a poll tax of $20 on Chinese entrants and the added requirement that no more than one Chinese passenger be carried for every ten tons of ship's burthen. The legislation was suspended in 1863, repealed in 1865, and re-enacted in 1881, with the tonnage ratio being increased to 1:100. The poll tax was dropped in 1888, but the legislation was made more restrictive by increasing the tonnage ratio to 1:500. In some colonies restrictions were more severe, although again not prohibitive; Queensland raised the poll tax to $60 in 1884, while New South Wales in 1888 raised the amount to $200, with a tonnage ratio of 1:300 (Price 1974; Markus 1979).

The legislation was not totally exclusive in a second sense. For much of the second half of the nineteenth century certain categories of Chinese were exempted from laws regulating immigration. The first definition of 'Chinese' adopted by the Victorian parliament in 1855 was pragmatic, designed to meet what was perceived to be an immediate problem, and only applied to males:

> the word 'Immigrant' shall mean any male adult native of China or its dependencies or of any islands in the Chinese Seas or any person born of Chinese parents (18 Vict., No. 39).

In 1857 the definition was further limited with the exemption of 'natural born or naturalized subjects of the Queen' (21 Vict., No. 42). Legislation in 1881 continued the exemption for British subjects (45 Vict., No. 723); in 1888, however, this was restricted to persons naturalised in the colony, and for the first time the notion of 'race' was introduced into the definition:

> 'Chinese' shall include every person of Chinese race not exempted from the provisions of this Act (52 Vict., No. 1005).

As in legislation dealing with Aborigines, the judiciary was empowered to decide, on the basis of physical appearance, whether a person was covered by the terms of the act (52 Vict., No. 1005, s.10).

There was considerable development of racial consciousness in the period 1850-90 and this is particularly apparent in legislation directed at the Chinese. With reference to the definition contained in legislation, there is a change from a territorial emphasis to one specifically couched in the terminology of race. There is also increasing acceptance of the idea of inequality, evident in the move to exclude designated groups from the mainstream of society. The objective of excluding Aborigines was readily apparent in the Victorian legislation of 1869, although this measure was not representative of developments in other colonies and was more typical of early twentieth century legislation. Discrimination against Chinese dates from 1855, but until the 1880s legislation was confined to the control of immigration and the activities of Chinese on the goldfields. Discriminatory measures in the 1880s began to assume a new character, directed towards a clear demarcation of the position of Chinese immigrants. Thus Chinese were denied the right of naturalisation in the late 1880s in New South Wales, Victoria and South Australia. In 1881 Victorian

Chinese who were not British subjects were denied the vote; a similar measure was enacted in South Australia in the following year and in 1885 Queensland denied the vote to 'an aboriginal native of Australia, India, China or the South Sea Islands... except in respect of a freehold qualification' (Price 1974:178).

While there was development of discriminatory legislation in the period 1850-1890, the process was far from completed. In all but two of the smaller colonies the target of legislation remained one specific group, and although immigration was controlled there was no total prohibition. Target groups were not defined solely on racial criteria; people of mixed Aboriginal-European descent, for example, continued to be defined with reference to mode of life. And the colonies were inconsistent in their attempts to exclude non-Europeans from the mainstream of society; thus Tasmania and Queensland did not abolish the right of naturalisation in this period.

The nature of these developments is further illustrated through an examination of categories employed by the colonial statisticians. There was a concern, beginning in the 1850s, to record the rate of Chinese immigration, their numbers and occupations, and also to estimate the number of Aborigines. But development beyond this point was slow; in this period there was no special attention given to refining categories in order to highlight the non-European presence. The tabulation of the 1881 Victorian census employed only three categories to summarise the population, namely, those exclusive of Chinese and Aborigines; Chinese; and Aborigines (Census 1881:123). The 'birthplaces of the people' were tabulated by country, not 'race', with a further distinction made between British possessions and the rest of the world. The major divisions were; Australasian colonies; United Kingdom; other British possessions (in Europe, Asia, Africa, America); European countries; Asiatic countries; African countries; American countries; and Polynesia. A footnote pointed out that in addition to the Chinese born in China there were an additional 329 persons of 'Chinese race' born elsewhere (Statistical Register 1883:7). The 1891 Victorian census employed similar divisions but, indicative of a growing willingness to adopt broad categories, the entry for Asiatic countries drew a distinction between the 17 persons born in China of European parents ('European race') and the 8,450 Chinese of 'Asiatic race' (Statistical Register 1892:8).

1890-1940

The third period, approximately dated from 1890 to 1940, witnessed the flowering of racial consciousness. Legislation was enacted to bar totally the permanent immigration of persons perceived to belong to certain racial groupings and to deny to those already in the country full enjoyment of

51

political rights and privileges. These actions were based on a fully articulated racial consciousness.

Late in the nineteenth century and early in the twentieth most states adopted legislation similar to the Victorian Act of 1869 which provided authority to remove Aborigines to reserves and to control all aspects of their lives, including terms of employment, control of assets, right of marriage and guardianship of children.

Legislation controlling immigration enacted in the same period was characterised by a move from specific to generic categories. Whereas in the past legislators dealt with perceived problems of an immediate, practical nature, they now strove to pre-empt their development by enacting legislation employing broad categories. Thus the New South Wales Coloured Races Restriction Bill of 1896 was directed at 'all persons belonging to any coloured race inhabiting the continent of Asia, or the continent of Africa, of any island adjacent thereto, or any island in the Pacific or Indian oceans'. A similar Bill was passed in Tasmania (Yarwood 1964; Charteris 1937). At the behest of the British government, subsequent legislation controlling immigration cloaked the specific target groups by adopting an education test, but there was little doubt that this test was to be applied in a discriminatory manner against non-Europeans, a point made clear in parliamentary debates and government memoranda (Yarwood, 1964). Most legislation outside the immigration field remained phrased in less circumspect terms. Thus, for example, the Post and Telegraphs Act of 1901 stipulated that only 'white labour' was to be employed in the carriage of mail on behalf of the Commonwealth (No. 12 of 1901, s.16(1)).

Australian governments were not content with halting non-European immigration; it was felt necessary to exclude non-Europeans - including Aborigines, as already noted - from the mainstream of community life, as well as subjecting them to discriminatory measures which denied them benefits normally available to taxpayers and restricted their job opportunities. The extreme example of this policy was the deportation in 1906 of most Melanesians resident in Australia (Corris, 1973). Other non-Europeans were allowed to remain, possibly because their deportation would cause serious diplomatic problems, but it was made clear that they were not wanted. In 1902 the Commonwealth disenfranchised any 'aboriginal native of Australia, Asia, Africa or the Islands of the Pacific except New Zealand', unless legislation in their state of residence conferred the vote (No. 8 of 1902, s.4). In 1903 the Commonwealth denied naturalisation to any 'aboriginal native of Asia, Africa or the Islands of the Pacific, excepting New Zealand' (No. 11 of 1903, s.5). Commonwealth legislation establishing old age and invalid pensions in 1908 disqualified Asiatics (unless born in Australia), and aboriginal natives of Australia,

Africa, islands of the Pacific and New Zealand (No. 17 of 1908, s.21). In 1912 the Commonwealth denied to 'women who are Asiatics, or are aboriginal natives of Australia, Papua, or the islands of the Pacific' (No. 8 of 1912, s.6).

Occupational discrimination dated from the late 1850s, the early targets being Chinese goldminers; subsequent discrimination affected storekeepers, hawkers, and Chinese working in the furniture trade. Such discrimination reached fullest development in the twentieth century, although with significant variation between the states. Queensland led the way, with one scholar identifying 40 discriminatory Acts in the period 1900-40; these measures covered the ownership and leasing of land, obtaining a loan from the Agricultural Bank, fishing for pearl shell and beche-de-mer, the manufacture of agricultural products, and employment in railway construction (Mercer 1981).

Some internal discriminatory measures also used the subterfuge of an education test, thus lessening the likelihood of diplomatic protests and simplifying the task of legislators who experienced difficulty in reaching a precise definition of the inferior races. Attempts at definition occasionally employed the concept 'white labour' but it was more common to attempt an enumeration of races, continents or geographical regions: presumably the legislators thought they were enumerating races, although this is not fully clear as the categories were rarely labelled as racial in legislation. These enumerated definitions contained a number of inconsistencies; thus in Commonwealth enactments Maoris were specifically exempted from the category of persons debarred from voting and citizenship, but they were specifically excluded from entitlement to pensions. Papuans were noted for the first time in a 1912 definition (No. 8 of 1912, s.6). 'Asiatics' born in Australia were deemed worthy of receiving the pension but not apparently the maternity benefit. There was, perhaps, a degree of logic in this discrimination: 'Asiatics' born in Australia would not be encouraged to have children, but as an act of magnanimity they would not be left destitute in old age.

This legislation of the early Commonwealth period signals a major development in racial consciousness, but it does not denote a termination point or full maturing. Racial consciousness without clear boundaries continued to undergo a process of development, with the definition of acceptable genetic stock being refined and narrowed. This development may be illustrated by examining the changing definition of Aborigine, government policy towards European immigration, and the categories employed by the Commonwealth statistician.

The 1897 Queensland definition of Aborigine was similar to that contained in the earlier Victorian Act, with the status of persons of mixed descent being determined by their mode of life or association. Those covered by the legislation were;

(a) an aboriginal inhabitant of Queensland; or
(b) a half-caste who, at the commencement of this Act, is living with an aboriginal as wife, husband or child; or
(c) a half caste who, otherwise than as wife, husband or child, habitually lives or associates with aboriginals (No. 17 of 1897).

This definition of 'half-castes' was subsequently developed to exclude consideration of social factors and to place reliance solely on supposed genetic inheritance. In deciding the eligibility of persons of mixed descent for social services and the franchise, and for inclusion in the census, the principal criterion was preponderance of non-Aboriginal 'blood' - there was some confusion whether preponderance meant 50% or 51% - although reference to mode of life was considered as a secondary factor. Thus a person defined as a 'half-caste' (i.e. non-Aboriginal by one Commonwealth criterion) who live on a reserve would not be eligible for a pension (Australian Archives 1938, 1949). Reference to mode of life finally disappeared from definitions adopted by some states in the 1930s, a time representing the high point of biological determinism in Australia. Western Australian legislation in 1936 was extended to cover persons of mixed descent, with exceptions for certain categories of 'quadroon', defined as 'a person descended from the full blood original inhabitants of Australia or their full blood descendants but who is only one-fourth of the original full blood' (No. 43 of 1936, s.2(f)). The definition of 'half-caste' in the Queensland Act of 1939 included a person

> Both of whose parents have a strain of aboriginal blood, and who himself has a strain of more than twenty-five per cent of aboriginal blood but who has not a preponderance of such blood... (3 Geo. 6, No.6).

The process of narrowing the category of acceptable racial stock is also illustrated by controls on European immigration in the 1920s. In 1901 potential immigrants had been placed in two categories: the admissable (Europeans) and the inadmissable (non-Europeans). In the 1920s the federal government adopted a third category, in line with misgivings concerning the suitability of certain European peoples: this category comprised immigrants who could only be admitted in strictly limited numbers, their entry being controlled by numerical quotas. Those affected included Maltese, Greeks, Yugoslavs, Albanians, Czechoslovaks, Poles and Estonians (Australian Archives, 1928). In the late 1930s the Commonwealth added the category of 'Jews', requiring all prospective immigrants to declare whether or not they were of the 'Jewish race'. Following a number of protests the government diplomatically changed the wording to require a person merely to declare if they were Jewish, deleting the reference to race (Markus 1983). During this period an officer of the Commonwealth Investigation Branch, in a highly unusual questioning of racial premises, inquired of his Director:

> Two dancers who are now appearing in Melbourne... have made applications [for permanent residence]... One is a Jewess married to an Aryan, member of the Church of England, and the other is a Roman Catholic Czech married to a Jewish man. To what race will their children belong? I recently asked a new arrival who looked 'German' rather than Jewish, whether she was a Jewess and a refugee. She told me her grandfather, who was a Prussian officer, married her Grandmother, a Jewess. Her father married a Jewess - what *race* is she? One generation behind her father, she was *Prussian*, - a Prussian, although applicant is not even German... If a Government officer 'thinks' a nominee is Jewish, where an applicant thinks he is not, where are we going to land? (Australian Archives 1939).

A third index to the development of racial consciousness - in particular the striving for precision and consistency - is provided by the questions asked in the census. In 1911 Australians were merely asked to indicate the race to which they belonged. At the next census in 1921 a tentative attempt was made to suggest categories: people were asked to state if they were of European race; if not, they were asked to indicate the non-European race to which they belonged. A further step in 1933 was the suggestion of categories for the non-Europeans:

> If of European race wherever born write European, if non-European state the race to which you belong as Aboriginal, Chinese, Hindu, Negro, Afghan, etc. If a half-caste write also 'H.C.' as 'H.C. Aboriginal', 'H.C. Chinese' etc.

This striving for greater precision was hindered by one small problem: the inability to formulate an acceptable racial taxonomy. Hence the statistician's resort to 'etc.' in his enumeration. In recording arrivals and departures, moreover, he seemed completely confused as to the meanings of 'nationality' and 'race'. Thus in 1925 one table listed Chinese and Japanese as 'nationalities', while the same categories - Chinese and Japanese 'nationalities' - were employed in a second table listing 'non-European races' (Year Book 1925:946-7). As a result of this inconsistency, in 1927, the category 'Nationality or Race' was adopted, a classic each way bet (Year Book 1927:899). In 1946 the information, using the same divisions (for example, Chinese and Japanese), was reclassified under the heading 'Racial Origin' (Year Book 1946-7:732).

From 1945 -
A fourth period, dating from the end of the second world war to the pre-

sent time, has witnessed a movement away from ideas of biological determinism and a decrease in the significance that governments attached to racial categories.

A basic feature of post-war development was the redefinition of the category of immigrants who could, first, be admitted without restriction and, second, be encouraged to migrate by the provision of assisted passages. A cognate development was the redefinition of persons who could be admitted to the full exercise of citizenship. Whereas the first forty years of the century witnessed a narrowing of categories, the reverse occurred in the post war period, so that practically all forms of discrimination were removed from the statute books and the Racial Discrimination Act of 1975 outlawed 'any act involving a distinction, exclusion, restriction or preference based on race, colour, descent or national or ethnic origin' (No. 52 of 1975, s.9).

An early change was the redefinition of desirable immigrants. Whereas southern and eastern Europeans had, in the pre-war period, been placed in the category of persons who could be admitted only in strictly limited numbers, from 1948 the immigration of previously undesirable national groups was encouraged, the category of acceptability being rapidly extended to meet the country's labour requirements (Markus 1984; Wilton and Bosworth 1984).

Paralleling this development was a change in policy towards Aborigines. Previously condemned to extinction on the margins of European society, Aborigines by the 1950s were expected to assimilate to white society, beginning with those of mixed descent. Signs of change were already apparent in the social welfare legislation of the 1940s. The Commonwealth's Child Endowment Act of 1941 provided for payment to Aborigines who were not nomadic or dependent on the Commonwealth or a state for support, thus indicating a move away from strict biological definition (No. 8 of 1941, s.15). In 1959 all Aborigines except those classed 'nomadic or primitive' were granted entitlement to pensions and maternity allowances, with this final discrimination being removed in 1966 (No. 51 of 1959, s.24; No. 41 of 1966, s.29). Legislation establishing unemployment and sickness benefits in 1944 did not automatically rule out Aborigines, but made their entitlement dependent on 'character, standard of intelligence and development' (No. 10 of 1944, s.19). This legislation was modified in 1959 and 1966 in line with modifications to other social service measures.

The states undertook a piecemeal repeal of legislation denying basic civil liberties to Aborigines, although at an uneven pace; Victoria removed barriers to full citizenship in 1957, New South Wales in 1963, South Australia in 1966 and Western Australia in 1972. The remaining vestiges of discriminatory Queensland laws were over-ridden by the Commonwealth's 1975 Aborigines and Torres Strait Islanders (Queensland Discrimination Laws) Act (No. 75 of 1975).

A third area of change involved non-Europeans born outside Australia. In 1950 war-time refugees resident in Australia were granted permanent residence, as were Chinese holding temporary entry permits who did not wish to return to their homeland following the victory of the communist forces. In 1956 the privilege of naturalisation was extended to certain non-Europeans, notably the wives and husbands of Australian citizens. Beginning in 1959 permanent residence was opened to 'distinguished and highly qualified Asians'; guidelines were further changed in 1966 to permit a larger intake of 'well qualified' non-Europeans, and to liberalise family reunion criteria and terms for naturalisation. The removal of remaining forms of racial discrimination was implemented in 1973 (Palfreeman 1967; Yarwood and Knowling 1982; Price 1983).

While immigration restrictions were gradually modified, leading to the removal of racial discrimination, and discriminatory measures against resident non-Europeans met a similar fate, the division of human populations into racial categories continues to the present time, albeit in a muted form. The social significance of racial categorisation, of ideas of racial determinism, lost legitimacy, but the categorisation itself retains its hold.

The Commonwealth statistician, for example, continued to seek greater precision in racial categorisation long after governments began the process of dismantling discriminatory legislation. Thus the 1947 census had instructed people of mixed descent to define themselves according to the race of their father. After nineteen years this instruction was found to be inadequate; thus in 1966 those of mixed descent were required to indicate the precise nature of admixture in fractional terms, as in ½ European - ½ Aboriginal, ¾ Aboriginal - ¼ Chinese'. The striving for data of supposedly greater precision ended in 1971 with those of mixed origin being requested merely to indicate the race to which they 'considered' they belonged. The race question was omitted in 1981, only to reappear in 1986.

Although continuing to collect information on the country's racial composition, the statistician had begun in 1961 to highlight possible deficiencies in the data, noting that 'The term "Race" as used for Census purposes is not synonymous with ethnic group, but is based on geographical rather than ethnological descriptions' (Year Book 1961:315). It was further observed in 1964 that 'The basic data do not permit scientific classification of ethnic origin and the races are named with a geographical rather than a truly ethnological description' (Year Book 1964:1303).

The publication of information on the race of immigrants was deleted after the 1958 Year Book; the racial composition of the population was deleted after 1967. Recording the elements of admixture in the Aboriginal population was the longest lasting obsession. It was lamented in 1973 that:

> reporting by Aborigines in the 1966 Census was insufficiently precise to differentiate persons who are 50 per cent Aboriginal from those who are more than 50 per cent Aboriginal... Even a total of all persons who are 50 per cent or more Aboriginal may be suspect, primarily because of the inclusion of persons who are less than 50 per cent Aboriginal and described themselves simply as 'Aboriginal', but also because of persons who are 50 per cent Aboriginal stating their race as 'European' (Year Book 1973:142).

The proportion of Aboriginal blood was last noted in the 1975-76 Year Book.

The quest for a definition of Aborigines has not, however, disappeared with changing perspectives and the dismantling of discriminatory legislation. In establishing entitlement to special benefit for Aborigines, governments have faced the continuing difficulty of defining eligibility. Since 1973 the Commonwealth has employed a definition for administrative purposes in which self-definition forms a constituent element. Eligibility is limited to:

> a person of 'Aboriginal' or 'Torres Strait Islander' descent who identifies as an Aboriginal or Islander and is accepted as such by the community with which he is associated (Year Book 1973:971).

In contrast with the agreed definition for administrative purposes, legislators have been unable to settle on a consistent form of words. In the period 1974-80, four different definitions appeared in federal Acts, at times directly contradicting each other. Thus in 1974 an Aborigine was defined as 'an indigenous inhabitant of Australia, and includes an indigenous inhabitant of the Torres Strait Islands' (No. 103 of 1974), yet a definition in the following year was restricted to 'a descendant of an indigenous inhabitant of Australia' and did not include a 'Torres Strait Islander' (No. 52 of 1975). Another attempt at definition in 1975 was premised on the existence of an 'Aboriginal race', but admitted doubt as to the classification of islanders; '"Aboriginal" means a person who is a member of the Aboriginal race of Australia. "Islander" means a person who is a member of the race to which Torres Strait Islanders belong' (No. 75 of 1975, s.3; No. 1 of 1977, s.3).

Concern with the precise degree of admixture is no longer a concern of legislators, but the validity of racial categorisation remains entrenched in-the law. The existence of races is unquestioned, although there is no agreed taxonomy and this leads to absurd attempts at definition. Nowhere is the assumption of validity more evident than in anti-discrimination legislation which outlaws acts based on 'race, colour, descent or national or ethnic origin', arguably serving to legitimise the misconception and bigotry that it is designed to counteract.

References

Australian Archives (1928), Immigration - Policy, CRS A458, P156/ 1.
Australian Archives (1938), Welfare of Aboriginals, CRS A571, 38/ 883.
Australian Archives (1939), Insp. R. Browne to Director, Attorney-General's Investigation Branch, 19 April 1939, CRS A367, C3075.
Australian Archives (1949), Aboriginals - Right to Vote, CRS A431, 49/ 822.

Broome, R. (1982), *Aboriginal Australians* Sydney, Allen and Unswin.
Census of Victoria, 1881, General Report.
Charteris, A. (1937), 'Australian immigration laws and their working', in N. MacKenzie (ed.) *The Legal Status of Aliens in Pacific Countries,* London, Oxford University Press.
Corris, P. (1973), *Passage, Port and Plantation* Melbourne University Press.
Evans, R., Saunders, K., Cronin, K. (1975), *Exclusion, Exploitation and Extermination* Sydney, ANZ Book Co.
Frost, A. (1981), 'New South Wales as *terra nullius:* the British denial of Aboriginal land rights' *Historical Studies* 77, 513-23.
Markus, A. (1979) *Fear and Hatred* Sydney, Hale and Iremonger.
Markus, A. (1983), 'Jewish Migration to Australia 1938-49' *Journal of Australian Studies* 13, 18-31.
Markus, A. (1984), 'Labour and Immigration 1946-9' The Displaced Persons Programme' *Labour History* 47, 73-90.
Mercer, P. (1981), 'The Survival of a Pacific Islander Population in North Queensland, 1900-1940', Ph.D. thesis, ANU.
Palfreeman, A. (1967), *The Administration of the White Australia Policy* Melbourne University Press.
Queensland Statutes
Price, C. (1974), *The Great White Walls are Built* Canberra, ANU Press.
Price, C. (1983), 'Immigration Restriction' in *The Australian Encyclopedia* 4th ed., vol. 5, Sydney, Grolier.
Reece, R. (1974), *Aborigines and Colonists* Sydney University Press.
Reynolds, H. (ed.) (1972), *Aborigines and Settlers* Melbourne, Cassell.
Rowley, C. (1970), *The Destruction of Aboriginal Society* Canberra, ANU Press.
Statistical Register of the Colony of Victoria, 1883, part II.
Statistical Register of the Colony of Victoria, 1892, part II.
Statutes of New South Wales
Statutes of Western Australia
Victorian Statutes
Wilton, J. and Bosworth, R. (1984), *Old Worlds and New Australia* Ringwood, Penguin.
Yarwood, A. (1964), *Asian Migration to Australia* Melbourne University Press.
Yarwood, A. and Knowling, M. (1982), *Race Relations in Australia* North Ryde, Methuen.
Year Book of the Commonwealth of Australia, 1908-1985.

Australian Aboriginal Studies: The Anthropologists' Accounts

Gillian Cowlishaw

Of all the groups in Australia designated in terms of race or culture none has had their authenticity questioned as much as Aborigines. Popular conceptions as well as academic writings make an implicit or explicit division of Aborigines into two kinds. They may be termed traditional and non-traditional, part-Aborigines and full-bloods or those in the north and those in the south (cf. Langton, 1981). One category is commonly seen as more legitimately Aboriginal. The popular view that the 'non-traditional' or 'half-castes' are not 'true' Aborigines is widely recognised, but anthropologists' complicity in such judgements is less obvious. There could be two reasons for such divisions. They could indicate that Aboriginal groups occupy such different structural positions in the wider society that they are not easily analysed within the same theoretical framework or by using identical research strategies. Alternatively, the Aborigines themselves could be perceived as so different racially or culturally as to preclude any analysis that encompasses both categories. This latter view has probably been the most pervasive both in anthropology and elsewhere, to the extent that the 'southern' or 'non-traditional' groups are sometimes denied inclusion in the category of Aborigines.

Neither argument can be easily sustained. The division would imply sharp contrasts between the history and culture of northern and southern Aborigines as well as shared unique features in each area. But there are numerous differences both in the nature of the Aboriginal groups themselves and in their relationships with the wider community. There are common themes in the history of the Northern Territory and southern Australia, and there are striking cultural and historical contrasts between communities in each area. The *de facto* separation of the literature on Aborigines into two major categories is a function of anthropological interest in both senses of the word.

I argue here that this dichotomy is misleading and has resulted from a narrow definition of the task of social anthropology. Only *some* features of *some* social groups are investigated. Although a number of contemporary anthropologists have recognised that the dichotomy is false it is still embedded in much writing, in terms such as 'part-Aboriginal' and 'of Aboriginal descent', and in the propensity of most anthropologists in Australia to work in the north of the continent. Ideas about anthropology which underlie this division have largely remained unexamined.

Three assertions will be the subject of this paper. Each is controversial in a different way and each is related to the history of anthropological thought and practice in Australia.

First, anthropologists in the 20th century have been influential in determining how Aboriginal society was understood by Australian intellectuals, politicians, journalists and now by the land courts (cf. Shiels, 1963). Second, the anthropologists' definition of Aborigines was always dependent on notions of their cultural integrity and homogeneity. No concepts or theories were developed within Australian anthropology which could adequately deal with either relations between the indigenous population and the invaders or with changes in either. Yet both of these were significant issues confronting field researchers wherever they worked. Finally, when anthropologists did conduct research with non-traditional groups the very vocabulary of 'caste' and 'blood' with which such groups were described, relied on *biological* ideas of race, and the search for the traditional also relies in the final analysis on the reification of race.

The concept of race as a way of dividing the human species into discrete groups was fundamental to the practice of anthropology during the 19th century. Aborigines were seen as a race, and the defining characteristics were to be discovered by measuring their bodies and bones. It was only in the mid 20th century that biologists resoundingly rejected racial categories by showing that variation within such groups is greater than variation between them. Where the average variation between groups is significant, only biologically superficial characteristics such as skin colour or hair type are involved. Throughout human history continuous migration has precluded the development of sub-species (Gould 1981:323).

But the biologists' rejection of racial categorisation of the human species did not eliminate the concept of race from popular or academic discourse. Instead of adopting the biologically more accurate term 'population' or 'gene pool', the term 'race' was retained. Social scientists asserted that it had a new meaning because it referred to a social rather than a biological category. However the defining features of the social category have not been the subject of analysis. Rather, it is my contention that social anthropologists uncritically equated 'traditional Aborigines' with the previous 'Aboriginal race', an equation which rendered the study of 'non-traditional', 'southern' or 'mixed race' groups anthropologically invalid.

Anthropology in Australia developed an institutional base with the establishment of the Australian Association for the Advancement of Science in 1888. In its first twenty years the anthropology section of this Association had, either as presidents or participants, the major anthropological researchers of the day - Howett, Fison, Roth, Gillen, Spencer, John Mathews and R.H. Mathews (Elkin, 1970:9). According to Elkin it was the 1914 meeting with anthropologists from the British Association for the Advancement of Science that forced offical and public recognition of anthropology in Australia. But there is no doubt that anthropology was flourishing before this; and the dominant intellectual currents of British thought directed anthropological research interests in this country. For instance, Fison and Howitt's *Kamilaroi and Kurnai* (1880) provided an example of the 'lowest level' of Morgan's kinship types. Baldwin Spencer gained Frazer's patronage on finding the most 'primitive' form of religion in Central Australia. Further, 'By the 1880's Darwin and Huxley had received awards and tributes from Australian Royal Societies, had their works included on Australian University syllabuses and had won complete hegemony over anthropological thinking' (Glover, 1982:18).

Although the physical character of Aborigines was studied by anatomists and craniologists, and the social character by a diverse range of people from surveyors and magistrates to medical officers and zoologists, both groups of researchers worked within the framework of evolutionary theory in which the major facts on the matter of race had already been decided. Some races were more developed than others. Even before theories of polygenesis and degenerationism gave way to unilinear evolutionary theory, there was virtually universal acceptance of the relative positions of the European and Australian types of humankind. The former was at the highest stage of development and the latter at the lowest. It only remained to show in what way and to what degree Aborigines were behind the development of other races. As Mulvaney says, 'In the polemics of nineteenth century evolutionary controversy, when men declared themselves for apes or angels, the Australians were ranged firmly on the side of the apes' (Mulvaney, 1969:12).

The work of physical anthropologists and those researching stages of social development proceeded in parallel. Around the turn of the century anatomists and craniologists spent a lot of time measuring skulls both inside (cranial capacity) and outside (cephalic index) as they were convinced that limited brain size was related to the supposed inferiority of Aborigines. Even after the relationship between brain size and intellectual ability had been dealt a severe blow in the 1880s, with the demonstration that some highly respected German Professors had smallish brains and some criminals large ones (Gould, 1981:93-4), the measuring continued for over sixty years in Australia (cf. Abbie 1957). The specific aims of this research did change, but the specifying of racial characteristics remained one major underlying theme of physical anthropology.

From the 1880s anthropologists aimed to show that the Australians could occupy one of the gradations between ape and man. Howitt was convinced that 'Australian evidence had proved the truth of evolutionary theory' (Glover, 1982:17). Baldwin Spencer speculated that, having been 'shut off from the competition of the higher forms, the Australian Aborigine is a relic of a type of mankind once widely scattered over the world' (Glover, ibid, 16). And Darwin used the Australian female as evidence in his argument that the difference between man and ape was one of degree, not of kind (Darwin, 1871:62).

There has been no thorough critique of the findings of early Australian anthropologists. Gould (1981) and Glover (1982) have shown that many who claimed to be objectively describing the characteristics of racial groups were already convinced that the black races were inferior. Gould's work shows conclusively that the measurement and ranking of human capacities, as a methodology, is subject to serious error and misunderstandings. It is not the measurements that are incorrect, but the meanings given to them, particularly the assumption that there could be some general measure on which human beings could be ranked in order of merit. What is significant for my purposes is that a century elapsed before the reasons for the error in this search were clearly set out. Gould's analysis of the general fascination with measurement, whether of intelligence quotients or skulls, is the first radical critique, not only of the measurements and their meanings, but of underlying suppositions about human variation which allows such research to flourish under the rubric of science. It is the twin fallacies of reification and ranking, first of races and more recently of IQs, that Gould identifies at the root of these endeavours.

For many years now there have been denials by anthropologists and biologists, of any necessary connection between biological race and physical, social or intellectual inferiority (e.g. Montagu, 1974). But, besides the work of George Stocking (1968), there has been little reassessment of the social anthropologist's heritage from evolutionary theory; many unexamined assumptions are still part of the framework of social anthropology. Glover (1982) begins his critique with a demonstration that not only physical anthropology but the early social anthropologists in Australia shared the view that their task consisted of tracing the tree of man and showing the features that were characteristic of particular-primitive societies. While the social anthropologist's interest in the position of Australians in the heirarchy of man waned with the advent of structural functionalism, the definitive characteristic of this 'unique people' remained the primary object of anthropological investigation. Despite the break between social and physical anthropology that occurred in the 1920s, there were conceptual continuities which I wish to question.

Gould says that 'Science cannot escape its curious dialectic. Embedded in surrounding culture, it can nonetheless be a powerful agent for question ing and overturning the assumptions that nurture it. Scientists can struggle to identify the cultural assumptions of their trade and to ask how answers might be formulated under different assertions' (1981:23). One 'cultural assumption' of social anthropology in Australia since the rise of structural functionalism concerns the submerged or implied definition of Aborigines as a race, the identification of that race with an unsullied tradition and the protection of this ever-narrowing category of Aboriginal studies from any systematic concern with the nature of the wider society or with changes in the object of investigation. In other words, although direct references to race were dropped, the concept of discrete *a priori* categories of human beings has remained central to the anthropological endeavour. This concept is, I would argue, isometric with the concept of race: that is, the concept of 'Aboriginal culture' has neatly filled the semantic space that 'Aboriginal race' previously occupied.

Questioning tradition is not a popular enterprise among the predominantly positivist 'Aboriginalists'. Recent attempts to re-examine the relationships between anthropology's past and anthropologists' practices have aroused defensive reactions (eg. A.A.S. Newsletters 1980-82). Thus I should make it clear that my discussion of the history and current practices of anthropology is not intended as a total rejection of the work of traditional anthropologists. Rather it is an attempt to develop a more informed and intelligent debate on those relationships. Some anthropologists believe that there is a sharp division between science and politics and that the former must be protected from the latter. I argue that anthropology in Australia is demonstrably related to the position of Aborigines in the wider society, not only in the more obvious ways, such as through the land rights movement, but the concepts and interpretations of Aboriginality have been developed through research conducted with the (white, European) discipline (e.g. Maddock, 1983; Hiatt, 1982; Gumbert, 1984). Decisions about funding the craniologist's search for evidence of the smaller Aboriginal skull in the 1880s are not different in principle from decisions taken in the 1980s about the funding of various other research projects. The kind of research that is encouraged in universities, the topics that are considered serious science and the work that is published are all part of a whole intellectual climate which has changed markedly in the last 100 years but, I would argue, is no less prone to error.

Some critics of anthropology have been accused of sentimentality or indulgence in partisan fervour (e.g. by Hiatt, 1983:54). They may more accurately be described as annoyed at the tendency to 'fiddle while Rome burns'. To have doubts about the fiddling entails no criticism of the violin. It is the priorities involved in allocating resources and energy to politically and intellectually dubious pursuits of ever more hopefully accurate information about a 'traditional' society that no longer exists, that arouses ire. I would not of course argue that anthropologists determine the degree of Aboriginal disadvantage in Australia today; only that they have diverted their attention from the analysis of the events that have produced that disadvantage. It is understandable if anthropologists become irritated or bored when accused of simply being products of their time. I want to show how their intellectual products have become effective perpetrators of the errors of their times.

From the second decade of the 20th century, British structural functionalism increasingly challenged the evolutionary framework of Australian anthropologists. Proto-anthropologists such as Howitt (Fison and Howitt, 1880) and Spencer (1904), and collectors of information such as Curr (1886) and Woods (1879), had sought comparative material, especially on kinship and religion, within in the framework of a unilinear evolutionary theory. The major break with these endeavours came when Radcliffe-Brown arrived as the first Professor of Anthropology at Sydney University in 1926. The increasing concern was then to delineate the internal structuring of the typical Aboriginal social group, and its variations across Australia. Comparative historical questions lost their urgency, and concern with the nature of races and racial difference became peripheral. Radcliffe-Brown expressed this break in a footnote to 'The Social Organisation of Australian Tribes':

> Practically all the theoretical discussion of Australian social organisation has been directed towards providing hypothetical reconstructions of its history... The more modest but really more important task of trying to understand what the organisation really is and how it works has been neglected (193:426).

From this time on there was a flowering of social anthropology (as it took a different direction from physical anthropology) and the establishment of a tradition of long field-trips for participant observation in one community: the results of these investigations were usually published in the journal *Oceania*. Written accounts of social organisation and religious ritual were largely descriptive rather than analytical, and in the *Oceania* field reports there was little discussion of the significance of observations in terms of competing sociological theories. Interpretation consisted largely of specifying the social function of observed practices and beliefs (Warner, 1937). Attention was overwhelmingly focussed on social behaviour among Australian Aborigines and how it could most accurately be described.

As the twentieth century advanced, ideas disseminated from these specialised studies of social anthropology increasingly informed popular notions about Aborigines. Social anthropologists largely dominated the task of defining who Aborigines were and how their special characteristics could be defined and explained. These characteristics were cultural, which meant that they pertained to social organisation (kinship and marriage), religious belief and practice. Origins and physical characteristics were dealt with in initial chapters in textbooks (Elkin, 1938 and later editions to 1964; R M & C M Berndt, 1964), but such treatment relied on earlier theories and evidence and was not an essential part of the description of Aboriginal social organisation.

The major changes in the direction of research necessitated some modification to already widely acclaimed work. Many of the earlier explanations for the patterns of kinship nomenclatures and religious ritual, in terms of stages in the unilinear development of human society, become an embarrassment. But rather than mounting a thorough going reassessment of the material gathered so far, researchers simply ignored the sections referring to stages of development and incorporated material gathered under an evolutionary paradigm into a new framework. For instance, in 1904 Spencer and Gillen published their study of *The Northern Tribes of Central Australia* which included the description of group marriage as an early (i.e. evolutionary) form of marriage. When this 19th century interpretation of marriage was generally rejected, the term that Spencer and Fillen had initially translated as 'wife' was given instead the meaning 'legitimate sexual partner': in the 1927 edition of the book the section on group marriage was modified accordingly. Thus the behavioural observations of 'group marriage' became a description of 'wife-lending'. Clearly there are dangers when such short-cuts are taken.

The loss of interest in defining racial characteristics and in comparative questions meant that anthropologists tended to refrain from examining the consequences of miscegenation for the definition of Aborigines. The interest in a particular kind of culture encouraged that which was traditional and which defined Aborigines encouraged students of anthropology to repair to remoter parts of the continent where miscegenation was less apparent. They continued the work of the earlier compilers of information, providing descriptive accounts and interpretations of the complexities and subtleties of kinship, religion and other aspects of traditional Aboriginal society that commanded international interest. Thus, while in most parts of the continent the Aborigines had learned a great deal (though not of course scientifically) about the anthropologists' culture, the anthropologists' interest was only in those Aborigines who had escaped, through geographical fortune, the direct invasion of their territory. In the closely settled areas where often large Aboriginal minorities were to be found, there was little interest expressed by anthropologists. However, what little there was provides crucial evidence of the continued reliance on racial categories.

The few studies done in northern and western New South Wales uncritically used the terms half-castes, part-Aborigines or civilised Aborigines (eg. Elkin 1935, Reay 1945). The method of study was the usual anthropological one of participant observation of a community as if it were a bounded and stable entity, despite the fact that these groups were reserve or fringe dwellers. This analytic strategy derived from a particular theory of traditional culture as exotic and unchanging; cultures can therefore be 'broken down' or 'lost' owing to changed circumstances. Those who bear the culture are not seen as adapting to changes, as making strategic or rational judgements or as actively striving for certain ends. In other words culture from this perspective is a set of traditional practices and rules to be found either in the thinking of the people or in their habits. When the culture is no longer appropriate to changed conditions the people get confused. This identification of Aborigines with certain cultural practices leads to many problems. Aborigines allegedly behave in certain ways; are they still Aborigines if they behave in other ways? Or do they behave in other ways because they are no longer Aborigines? The terminology in these studies indicates raw confusion: reference to racial categories, half-castes and mixed bloods were made without any explanation of the relevance of 'caste' and 'blood' to what were supposedly studies of culture. There was thus an implied causal connection between the dilution of the blood and the loss of Aboriginal, that is traditional, cultural practices. Some indications of the origin of this elision of categories can be gained from an examination of early statements about the task of anthropology in Australia. The consequences are apparent in textbooks as I indicate below.

The anthropological endeavour was spelt out by Radcliffe-Brown in the first volume of *Oceania* in 1930. Anthropology was to be carried out 'by scientists who have been specially trained for the purpose' (Radcliffe-Brown, 1930:1). The science could be of practical value in the 'satisfactory control, in administration and education of what are called backward peoples, which require a thorough understanding of their culture' (1930:2). But, he added, 'These investigations are perhaps not of any immediate practical use, for the Australian aborigines, even if not doomed to extinction as a race, seem at any rate doomed to have their cultures destroyed' (1930:3). Firth, who was Professor of Anthropology and editor of *Oceania* for one year after Radcliffe-Brown left, indicated the kind of theory which underlay the usefulness of anthropology when he said that the principle of substitution, 'or replacing an item of culture which is ill-adapted to a new situation by one which is better fitted to stand the strain, is advocated by modern anthropology' (1931:4). Some attempts to show the use of anthropology to administrators of various kinds read like efforts to placate critics or justify funding, but Firth says there is also a

mass of information to be collected from the remnants of surviving

tribes in many portions of the continent who have been more influenced by white civilization ... Such work needs to be done soon, ere the
still primitive tribes lose the fresh vigour of their social and religious
system, and those already attached to the skirts of the white man loosen
their enfeebled grasp and go to join their elders (1932:6).

Firth's poetic bent should not obscure the very simple theoretical approach which is empiricist, functionalist and contrasts the Aborigine's
culture with the white's civilisation.

Firth recognises that 'it is inequitable and unsatisfactory to expect
aborigines to live their normal lives when removed from their ancestral
lands' (1932:10). This is the first reference to the issue that Elkin was to
stress repeatedly in future years, and it is Elkin's information that Firth is
referring to when he says the Aborigine 'cannot perform the rites which he
thinks give him his food and certainly give him a sense of well-being in an
alien land' (1931:10).

Elkin in 1938, R.M. & C.H. Berndt in 1964 and Maddock in 1972 published
the major anthropological text books on Aborigines. While markedly different, each also shows the confusion of culture with racial categories, and
each also invokes the static and mentalist notion of culture that drew the
same kind of boundaries that race had previously done. Elkin, above all
other anthropologists, wanted to help the Aborigines but did not examine
the institutions that were most directly oppressing them, particularly the
Aborigines' Protection Board. I am not saying that Elkin ignored the
A.P.B., but that his efforts on behalf of Aborigines did not involve any
analysis of the A.P.B's social function and cultural context. European institutions were not the focus of the anthropologists' studies: Aborigines'
characteristics were and on this topic the anthropologist was an expert,
although Elkin was never sure whether their intellects were inferior to
those of Europeans (1937). He berated those who, with narrow reasoning,
denied the Aborigines the opportunity of special instruction, and pointed
to the efficacy of such instruction given by the Americans in the Philip-
pines. He accepted that Aborigines had shown little power to adapt
themselves to our culture, but argued that 'the social and racial handicaps
... must be borne in mind' (1937:497). His major work, *The Australian
Aborigines; How to Understand Them* (first published 1938), had an initial
chapter on 'their human classification and place of origin' although the major part of the book is a detailed description of social organisation and
religious life. In the final chapter a section entitled 'A cultural hiatus'
describes Aborigines in the early settled districts who were mainly of mixed decent:

Their knowledge of Aboriginal language, customs, beliefs and sacred
places is, with few exceptions, fragmentary, though they often retain a

feeling of belonging to certain tribal areas, and experience the warmth and refuge of kinship and extended family ties. Aboriginal culture for them ... is no longer a steady flowing stream of knowledge, law and faith, coming from the 'ever present past' and remaining with them 'from one generation to another'. *And no other culture has taken its place...* Full-bloods in the northern and west-central regions still have their own living culture to give them firm and well-known ground on which to stand and face the future (1974:379, 381 my emphasis).

Elkin envisages the part-Aborigines as either sitting at the feet of knowledgable old full-bloods, it that is possible, or,

With their increasing opportunities of secondary and tertiary education, they may read and ponder on the records and expositions of Aboriginal culture made by anthropologists... In this way Aborigines, irrespective if caste, may become proud of their full-blood ancestors and gain an insight into the latter's philosophy of, and guide-lines to, life. Thus equipped, they will make their several ways more assuredly in the general Australian community, or in their own regional communities as long as these remain (1974:382).

Culture for Elkin then, is useful baggage which can be passed on in a number of ways; its loss leads to 'a kind of "culture non-existence"'(1974:381).

The next major general text was Catherine and Ronald Berndt's *The World of the First Australians* (first published 1964). Again, the first chapter covered origin and physical characteristics, and the bulk of the work described social organisation, material culture, the life cycle and religion. The final two chapters discuss 'what has been happening in the *non*-traditional sphere' (1977, ix, emphasis in the original).

The authors argue that 'the rapid disorganisation and relatively easy collapse' of the 'integrity and independence' of Aboriginal society was partly due to its 'heavy emphasis on non-change' and the fact that Aborigines on all counts 'were a conservative people' (1977:492). It is ironic that this depiction of Aboriginal society as unable to cope with change, because of a stress on permanence, which is echoed in many more popular works (eg. Stanner, 1969), is at least partly a consequence of anthropologists' methods of analysis. Their accounts of the characteristic institutions and ideologies of a society tend to emphasise stability over time. This stability, permanence or conservatism implies a comparison which is never spelt out.

It is possible to discern in the Berndts' text a similar idea about the nature of culture to that given by Elkin before, and Maddock after, them. After saying that 'Wherever Europeans settled in any numbers, the trend was the same. The Aborigines around them began to die out' (1977:506), they explain that the

> ... survivors were beginning to adopt some European ways, at least superficially. And there was a growing number of half-castes, offspring of European or other alien fathers and Aboriginal mothers. This dual process has continued all through the southern part of the Continent: diminishing 'Aboriginality', in physical as well as in cultural traits; and on both these scores a growing resemblance to Europeans (sic) (1977:506).

As for the 'traditionally oriented', the Berndts say they are harder to find than a few years ago but this 'is not to say that traditional elements will cease to survive in some form or other, but that Aboriginal life, as a way of life, will have ceased to exist' (1977:514), and furthermore, 'Aboriginality, on an Australia wide basis means no more than a common identification in physical terms, the accident of Aboriginal descent' (1977:515). The confusion shown here about biology and culture is not reduced by the assertion that the 'last great socio-cultural reservoirs, so to speak, have been Arnhem Land and the Western Desert' (1977:521). It appears then that these authors have written about a people whose identity is, they believe, fading away. A careful reading of their final chapters reveals no coherent explanation for this change although it is implied that the process is a natural consequence of the presence of Europeans.

Maddock did not begin his text *The Australian Aborigines* (first published 1972) with origins and physical characteristics, but with a statement in the preface that he would confine himself to 'what was living in Aboriginal tradition' although 'reference has been made to what is dead where that seemed necessary for the explication of what survives' (1982, viii). It is not clear where he found 'what was dead' but we can presume it was from anthropological texts rather than the memories of informants, and it can be inferred that what was living were ideas sometimes expressed in practices. The object of writing the book was to 'state some of the general features of Aboriginal society' and the author clearly believes that Aboriginal society only exists in the north of Australia. It is identified with a particular tradition, even though Maddock accepts that the tradition may be changed to some degree. He sees various 'cults' as ways that Aborigines have tried to better their conditions of life,

> ... while keeping at least some of their traditional culture. Indigenous symbols and ways of thought continued to be vital even when mixed with new ingredients. By envisaging distinctiveness for themselves, whether alongside or in place of whites, the followers of these movements refused to accept that their society was dying. Yet their enterprise must be seen as deluded in each case: either it appealed to powers that are not of this world or it proposed a most unlikely ex-

change. Although movements of this kind can keep up the spirit of their adherents, and thus help sustain the integrity of Aboriginal communities, their methods and assumptions are too fanciful for them to be able to tackle the real causes of the misery against which they are reacting. There is something self-defeating about a message that has to be deciphered by anthropologists (1982:9-10).

Maddock's account of Aborigines' response to the European challenge shows little appreciation of the dynamics of resistance. Nor does he explain his view of 'the real causes' of their misery, or how vital 'indigenous symbols' become part of a 'deluded' enterprise. He does say that 'open resistance could not last long; it was soon suppressed. Native interests were ranked so low in comparison with settler interests that they practically vanished from view and Aboriginal discontent was left to express itself in cryptic and ambiguous forms' (1982:10).

Though presenting what he defines as Aboriginal society in a very different light from Elkin and Berndt, Maddock nonetheless shares with those authors certain assumptions about the nature of 'traditional culture'. They each 'accord a critical priority to systems of human meanings [and]... leave unposed the question of how different forms of discourse come to be materially produced and maintained as authoritative systems' (Asad, 1979:619). That is, when Maddock says that indigenous ways of thought continued to be vital 'even when mixed with new ingredients' he is creating a recipe for confusion. Would it be possible to identify an 'indigenous way of thought' and specify the nature of the new ingredients and the reason for their being added? Why do these mixtures only raise 'the spirit of their adherents' and not anything more substantial? Are we perhaps in the realm, not of harmless metaphor, but of anthropological mythology and its mystifying symbol of the pure traditional culture?

The theory of culture used by these anthropologists included the view that after what was called 'culture contact' Aborigines began to 'lose' their culture. Given such theoretical orientations, Talal Asad has argued that 'the main trouble with much colonial anthropology ... and with much contemporary anthropology too ... has been not its ideological service in the cause of imperialism, but its ideological conception of social structure and of culture' (1979:624). He asserts that the difficulties anthropologists encountered in conceptualising social change stem from their preoccupation with essential human meanings. These 'authoritative meanings' tend to be for anthropologists the *a priori* totality which defines and reproduces the essential integrity of a given social order. That is, for anthropologists, culture is a particular ideology. The depiction of contemporary Aboriginal society has therefore been inadequate partly because it is difficult to recognise a systematic and consistent ideology among subordinate groups who lack the power to give authoritative expression to their ideas. An il-

71

lustration of the problem is Maddock's view that 'conditions in some Australian states are more compatible than ever before with the surviving features of traditional Aboriginal society' (1982 preface). I believe he is referring to the fact that reserve life allows more time for the performance of ritual than did station work. Thus rituals are 'surviving features' of what is, by implication, dead. In the Australian literature references to the culture being 'destroyed', 'undermined' or 'dislocated' are still common. Instead of any analysis of the processes of change we have such metaphoric phrases as 'upsetting the delicate balance between man and land', or 'the rapid collapse of traditional culture'.

Many of the studies done in the 1940s and 1950s in New South Wales and southern Queensland would be rejected as inadequate today. For instance, one researcher stated that work on reserves was useful because there were 'old people to whom the past was more real than the present with its disintegration of native social life' (Kelly, 1935:463), and the study concluded with the comment that 'research among the remnants on settlements is quite worthwhile' (1935:473). A more sophisticated author in the same tradition argued that 'when new beliefs and behaviour-patterns are adopted, and others inherent in the original culture remain, it is dangerous to attempt to define too sharply the separate spheres of influence of the older culture which has been rapidly declining and the new one which has been grafted on to it' (Reay 1949:89).

Here the two cultures apparently exist independently and people behave in terms of either one or the other. A common feature of such analysis is that Aborigines act in terms of their culture and that when it is 'lost' or 'eroded' they cannot 'adapt'. There is no attempt to understand how Aboriginal groups themselves responded and defined their aims in new contexts, nor how their choices were systematically expressed or limited, organised or suppressed. Elkin's work for instance on 'southern' Aboriginal groups was very much a response in terms of common-sense welfare notions accepted uncritically from his own cultural background. Maddock's only mention of Aborigines in the south is an assertion that 'in some regions there is scarcely any difference between Aborigines and other Australians' (1982:6) which, in my opinion, is simply superficial nonsense (cf. Beckett, 1958a; Cowlishaw, 1986). In general, the few studies conducted in the settled parts of Australia by anthropologists showed little appreciation of the historical, political and economic forces that had created the community being studied. Nor was there systematic attention paid to the way these Aboriginal communities were, in the contemporary situation, bounded by laws and practices that confined their activities to certain limited areas, both geographically and socially.

In the light of this dominant but restricted intellectual framework, the reason for the limited number of studies of the southern Aborigines is apparent. Aborigines in New South Wales and other settled parts of Australia no longer displayed that most definitive characteristic, their traditional culture. These southern studies are also accorded low status. One researcher has even said that working in New South Wales was seen as a kind of apprenticeship carried out by those not yet ready for the real anthropological work. It is apparent that the inadequacy of the conceptual framework anthropologists used in these studies is due to the limitation of their concept of culture which was still closely associated with the older concept of race. But it is important to recognise that the study of 'traditional' culture suffered from the same conceptual limitations. There are a number of reasons for this.

Australian anthropologists remained more concerned with their place in the international anthropological fraternity than concerned with analysing events in Australian society, although dramatic changes in the Aborigines' social positions were taking place, both through the economic development of those areas which had been the remote haven of 'traditional' Aborigines, and also in legislation. Even if they did not have a direct effect on isolated groups, these changes would eventually alter and to a large extent determine their futures. But no attention was paid to this fact either as the subject of research or, perhaps most seriously, as requiring methodological attention. Given, for instance, that the hunter-gatherers were no longer hunting and gathering but were fencing and mustering, was the researcher still collecting information about hunters and gatherers? How did the field workers on government settlements or missions determine what represented the past and what represented some adjustment to changed concitions? No discussion of this issue was initiated. It seems that most field workers simply relied on the idea that people, or at least traditional Aborigines, did not change their ideas and habits quickly. Under certain circumstances, such an assumption may not lead to serious distortion, although in others there is evidence to the contrary (cf. Reynolds 1981; Morris 1983; Anderson 1983). Anthropologists' major concerns were usually with those things which had not changed, and the use of the ethnographic present in anthropological accounts is convention which allows the writer to pretend that it is possible to observe, and even participate in, an unchanging society. My objection is less to the use of such a convention than to the lack of critical assessment of its effect.

I have argued that the only integrity recognised in an Aboriginal society, until recently at least, was the integrity of tradition. Yet a whole body of literature in anthropology, valuable as it is in recording past traditions, did not see itself as *simply* recording past traditions. Rather, it saw itself defining what Aborigines were, and are. This literature is dominated by the false notion that there *are* traditional Aboriginal societies.

73

The recently coined term, 'traditionally oriented' papers over a crack in the whole conceptual edifice, for it allows for the retention of the anthropologist's notion of culture as a stable set of ideas and practices that are peculiar to Aborigines and which define Aborigines. In the last ten years there has been an increasing number of anthropological studies of change in Aboriginal society, but the notion of a past cultural integrity that is being breached or altered is often a fundamental part of the theoretical framework (cf. Berndt 1977). Another approach presents the contemporary community, though demonstrably embattled and precarious, as if it were a self-managing entity in the classic field work style (e.g. Kolig, 1980; Sansom 1980). I will suggest later that there are more useful strategies possible, such as seeing culture itself as a living response to stable or chaning conditions.

Theories that continue to define Aborigines in terms of one tradition and ignore the social contexts in which racial boundaries and definitions are culturally constructed and reproduced will remain inadequate. The problem is a conceptual one concerning the category Aboriginal, but it is not one confined to anthropological discourse. Confused terminology and embarrassment often occur as people try to avoid imputing greater or less legitimacy to some Aborigines than others (cf. Reay, 1964; Tugby, 1975). My aim here is to escape this confusion which we inherited from a particular kind of theory of culture and its unacknowledged links with popular racial categories. If the study of race was the science that many of our academic forebears produced, which explained and thereby justified the differences between the colonisers and the colonised, could it not be argued that social anthropology, by defining Aborigines as have a particular unique and unchanging culture, has done the same thing?

We need to keep in mind the lessons from the earlier literature on the nature of racial differences: the concept of race which referred to discrete human groups was based on a biological error, and yet was used to assert inferiority. I am now suggesting that any connections between the specific characteristics of traditional Aboriginal culture and the political predicament of Aboriginal groups today are also invalid. Yet, it is the work of anthropologists that has invited such an explanation, even when they have not made the connection implicitly or explicitly themselves (cf. Berndt 1982: preface). In addressing this legacy, Morris has argued that 'The view that traditional practices and attitudes provided an insurmountable barrier to Aboriginal employment is simply misleading' and that 'creative adaptation is a form of culture change for a people who *had to depend* on their creativity and innovation to survive' (1983:511. Morris' emphasis).

It also ill behoves anthropologists to create a temporal division of culture. Aborigines may have never been quite as we have described them and, more seriously, we would have to explain when Aboriginal culture ceases to exist. Maddock has implied that he can tell, but many Aborigines are denied inclusion in his category. In contrast to these problems, it is refreshing to see a new dynamic approach emerging: two articles appeared recently in the same issue of Mankind (1983), both by young anthropologists critical of past accounts of Aborigines. Anderson attacks the new historians for their lack of recognition of culture and Morris attacks the old anthropologists for recognising nothing else. Both incorporate particular historical events in their explanations of the changing nature of the Aboriginal communities they are analysing.

The history of the literature on Aborigines is the history of anthropological hegemony and in the recent contributions from educationalists, historians, psychologists and political scientists, there is a tendency to rely on anthropologists' work for authoritative statements concerning Aboriginal traditions. It seems important therefore to define the limits of the anthropologist's area of expertise and admit that the discipline has no special authority in the area of what is called 'social change' or in the analysis of the kind of society into which Aborigines have been incorporated. The bulk of social anthropology in Australia on Aboriginal society until recently may be more accurately described as social archaeology.

In conclusion, I suggest a more useful approach for anthropological enterprise. In recent years the work about Aborigines has produced three themes. First, that Aborigines are victims of racism. Second, that Aborigines are victims of capitalism, exploited and dependent. Third, the theme of Aboriginal resistance to invasion and European hegemony. It is the third theme that seems to me to leave room for a more useful conception of culture and for analysing changes in Aboriginal society. Until a decade ago there was almost no recognition of the active part that Aborigines might have played in the retention or resurgence, or even rejection, of cultural forms as strategies in a political struggle. Quite the opposite. As indicated, Aborigines were usually depicted either as having lost their culture, or as clinging rather pathetically to its remains. But there is quite a different interpretation of such clinging, or indeed of rejection of particular traditions. The work of Gilroy in the United Kingdom develops a view of culture as essentially political. He says

> The struggles of 'black' people appear in an intensely cultural form because the social formation in which their distinct political traditions are now manifest has constructed the arena of politics on ground overshadowed by centuries of metropolitan capitalist development, thereby denying them recognition as legitimate politics.

He goes on to point out that the terms such as coon and wog (or boong), are cultural constructions in an ideological struggle, and that

[c]ultures of resistance develop to contest them and the power they inform, as one aspect of the struggle against capitalist domination which blacks experience as racial oppression. This is a class struggle *in* and *through* race (Gilroy 1981:210, emphasis in original).

He therefore argues that culture is a terrain of class conflict. Whether one accepts the class nature of the conflict or not, my major point is that this is a quite different way of viewing culture from the old tradition-retained-or-lost one. If culture is a creation, an expression of a human group's responses to their social existence, then the changing conditions of that existence does not mean a loss of culture. One could as well lose one's biology. Rather it means a cultural response to a different situation. That is, the Aboriginal response to change is cultural by definition. While Aborigines have not chosen the weapons or the arena on which the struggle is played out, nonetheless they have, consciously or unconsciously, continually responded to and resisted the hegemony of white society.

In New South Wales country towns there *is* an Aboriginal culture. There is an ongoing recreation of a distinct cultural heritage which has its own vocabulary, its family form, pattern of interpersonal interaction and even its own economy (Cowlishaw, in press). One source of this culture has been the specific everyday experience of the black population which has given rise to commonsense (in the Gramscian sense) ideas which conflict with the whites' commonsense concerning normality, propriety and the sanctity of private property. One of its manifestations is the highly developed humour which reinterprets events which threaten to engulf Aborigines' lives. Another part of it is the direct attacks on property. It is also manifested in the black power vocabulary which has been adopted by some of the young people, and in defiant public emphasis on values that are known to upset the dominant whites (cf. Young, N.D.; Beckett, 1958b). Willis and Corrigan (1983) have discussed such 'oppositional culture' in Britain, and the work of Genovese (1975) discusses equivalent cultural creations of the oppressed.

It is my contention that it is not the task of social scientists to define who is and who is not an Aborigine, or to pronounce on how far a community conforms to some typical or traditional form of Aboriginal society. The interest in such questions, and more recently in Aboriginality, stems from the dynamics of a racially divided society where a particular category of people has been subject to formal and informal sanctions since the arrival of Europeans. Neither biological nor cultural criteria can be used to distinguish, once and for all, a category of people called Aborigines, any more than set characteristics can identify Greeks, Americans or Chinese. Such groupings of people are made according to historically changed criteria and they gain social and political importance for historically specific reasons. Thus Aboriginality has become an important issue for

Aborigines today because of the political, economic and ideological position they are in.

Thus I argue that the Aborigines in the north, south, east and west of Australia are themselves defining what Aborigines are. Aboriginal culture is being changed, developed and extended in embattled situations. There has not been simply an attempt to cling to a past tradition but, wittingly or not, the creation of new ones. Part of the Aborigines' struggle today is over who is to define the very category 'Aboriginal'.

Notes

1. A notable exception is the work of Jeremy Beckett at Wilcannia (1958a).

Bibliography

Australian Anthropology Society Newsletters 1980 to 1982, Nos. 8 to 17.
Abbie A.A. (1957) Metrical characters of a central Australian tribe, *Oceania* 27(3) 220-248.
Anderson C. (1983) Aborigines and Tin Mining in North Queensland, *Mankind* 13 (6) 473-498.
Asad T. (1979) Anthropology and the Analysis of Ideology, *Man* (N.S.) 14, 607-627.
Van Den Berghe (1981) *The Ethnic Phenomenon,* New York, John Wiley.
Beckett J. (1958a) A Study of a Mixed Blood Minority in the Pastoral West of N.S.W., M.A. Thesis, A.N.U. Canberra.
Beckett J. (1958b) Aborigines Make Music, *Quadrant,* 8.
Berndt R.M. & C.H. (1977) *The World of the First Australians* (first published in 1964), Sydney, Ure Smith.
Berndt R.M. (ed) (1977) *Aborigines and Change,* Canberra, Australian Institute of Aboriginal Studies.
Berndt R.M. (ed) (1982) *Aboriginal Sites, Rights and Resource Development,* University of Western Australia Press.

Burridge K. (1973) *Encountering Aborigines,* New York, Pergamon Press.

Cowlishaw G.K. (1983) Blackfella Boss: A study of a Northern Territory cattle station, *Social Analysis,* 13.

Cowlishaw G.K. (1986) Race for Exclusion, *Australian and New Zealand Journal of Sociology, 22(1).*

Curr E.M. *(1886, 1887) The Australian Race,* Vols. 1-3, London & Melbourne, John Ferres. Govt. Printer.

Darwin C. (1871) *The Descent of Man,* London, John Murray.

Elkin A.P. (1935) Civilized Aborigines and Native Culture, *Oceania* 6(2) 117-46.

Elkin A.P. (1937) Native Education with Special Reference to the Australian .Aborigines, *Oceania* 7, (4) 459-500.

Elkin A.P. (1970) The Journal 'Oceania': 1930-1970, Sydney *Oceania Monograph* No. 166.

Elkin A.P. (1974) *The Australian Aborigines,* Sydney, Angus and Robertson (first published in 1938 with subtitle 'How to understand them'. Later editions 1943, 1954, 1964).

Firth R. (1931) Anthropology and Native Administration, *Oceania* 2, (1) 1-8.

Firth R. (1932) Anthropology in Australia 1926-1932-and after, *Oceania* 3(1).

Fison L. and Howitt, A.W. (1880) *Kamilaroi and Kurnai, The Netherlands* Anthropological Publications.

Genovese E. (1975) Class, culture and historical process, *Dialetical Anthropology* 1, 71-79.

Gilroy E. (1981) You can't fool the youths ... race and class formation in the 1980s, *Race and Class* XX111(2/ 3).

Glover R. (1982) Scientific Racism and the Australian Aboriginal 1865-1915: The Logic of Evolutionary Anthropology. B.A. Honours thesis, University of Sydney.

Gould S.J. (1981) *The Mismeasure of Man,* New York, Norton.

Gumbert M. (1984) *Neither Justice Nor Reason,* University of Queensland Press.

Hartwig M. (1972) Aborigines and Racism: an Historical Perspective, in F. Stevens (ed.) *Racism; The Australian Experience,* Vol. 2, Sydney, A.N.Z. Book Co. 9-24.

Hiatt L. (1982) Letter to the Editor. *Oceania* 52(3).

Hiatt L. (1983) Reply to Dr Cowlishaw. *Australian Aboriginal Studies,* 1, 53-54.

Kelly T. (1935) Tribes of Cherburg Settlement, Queensland. *Oceania* 5(4).

Kolig E. (1980) Noah's Ark revisited: On the myth-land connection in traditional Aboriginal thought, *Oceania* 51.

Langton M. (1981) Urbanising Aborigines: the Social Scientist's Great Deception. *Social Alternatives* 2(2) 16-22.

Maddock K. (1983) *Your Lord in Our land; Aboriginal Land Rights,* Ringwood, Penguin Books.

Morris B. (1983) From Underemployment to Unemployment. *Mankind* 13)6) 499-516.

Montagu A. (1974) *Man's Most Dangerous Myth; the Fallacy of Race.* Oxford University Press.

Mulvaney J. (1969) *The Prehistory of Australia,* London, Thames and Hudson.

Radcliffe-Brown A.R. (1930) Editorial, *Oceania* 1(1) 1-4.

Radcliffe-Brown A.R. (1930-31) The Social Organisation of Australian Tribes, parts 1-3. *Oceania* 1. 1-4, 34-63, 206-246, 322-341, 426-456.

Reay M. (1945) A Half-caste Aboriginal Community in North-Western New South Wales, *Oceania* 15(&) 296-323.

Reay M. (1949) Native Thought in Rural New South Wales. *Oceania* 20(2) 89-118.
Reay M. (1964) *Aborigines Now.* Angus and Robertson.
Reynolds H. (1981) *The Other Side of the Frontier* Queensland, James Cook University.
Rowley C. (1972) *Outcastes in White Australia,* Ringwood, Penguin Books.
Sansom B. (1980) *The Camp at Wallaby Cross,* Canberra, Australian Institute of Aboriginal Studies.
Shiels H. (ed) (1963) *Australian Aboriginal Studies,* Oxford University Press.
Spencer W.B. & Gillen E.J. (1904) *The Northern Tribes of Central Australia,* London, MacMillan.
Spencer W.B. & Gillen E.J. (1927) *The Arunta,* Vols 1 & 2, London, MacMillan.
Stanner W.E.B. (1969) *After the Dreaming,* Australian Broadcasting Commission.
Stevens F.S. (1984) *Aborigines in the Northern Territory Cattle Industry,* Canberra A.N.U. Press.
Stocking G. (1968) *Race, Culture and Evolution,* New York, Free Press.
Tonkinson R. (1978) *The Marudjara Aborigines; Living the Dream in Australia's Desert,* New York, Holt, Rinehart and Winston.
Tugby D. (1973) *Aboriginal Identity in Contemporary Australian Society,* Brisbane, The Jacaranda Press.
Warner L. (1937) *A Black Civilization,* New York, Harper.
Willis P. and Corrigan P. (1983) Orders of Experience: Working Class Cultural Forms, *Social Text,* 7, 8-103.
Woods J.E. (1879) *The Native Tribes of South Australia,* Adelaide E.S. Wigg.
Young Dougie (n.d.) Wilcannia folk songs - Recordings by J Beckett held at Australian Institute of Aboriginal Studies.

Racism and Sexism in Australian National Life

Marie de Lepervanche

In most discussions on racism - whether these concentrate on definitions, on the origins or history of racism, its association with capitalism, immigrant labour, nationalism or even with right wing politics - there is very little mention of the complex relation between racism and sexism. The exceptions in Australia are in a few sociological writings (Collins, 1984) and within the feminist literature (Curthoys, 1975; Gordon, 1975; Saunders, 1982; Aveling, 1985). Gordon's comments provide an example;

> The oppression of women is closely interwoven with notions of race. In Australia... the desire for a high birthrate and the maintenance of racial strength and purity have long been national priorities... Concomitant with the cry 'to populate or perish', the decimation and containment of Aborigines and the exclusion and restriction of non-white immigrants, has been the confinement of women to their reproductive functions. White women in Australia have been viewed primarily as breeders of the Anglo-Saxon strain... (Gordon, 1975:40).

There is plenty of evidence to support Gordon's claim although many women have resisted these patriarchal demands.

Usually, the implicit if not explicit assumption underlying most analyses is that the perpetrators and victims of racism include men and women equally. To some extent that assumption holds, in certain circumstances and from certain viewpoints. For example, after 1901 white mean *and* women in Australia contributed to the consensus over the White Australia Policy. Likewise, this policy excluded both male and female non-Europeans: but for those non-European males already domiciled here there were extra restrictions forbidding entry to their wives and children. There were also other important differences: when we consider the imagined communities of both 'race' and 'nation' (cf. Anderson, 1983), women's social position in each differs from men's.

Women in general have been subjected to a double structural load of inequality insofar as they have been associated with dependent, domestic reproduction and have been commonly designated the consumers, while men have held sway in the public world of production and, if white, in politics. More particularly, insofar as race is concerned, women have also been prone to ideological slippage. Men keep shoving them across cultural boundaries when it suits them. In the male rhetoric of racism (and nationalism) women have occupied diverse positions all of which have sexist implications.

For example, when indentured coloured labour was introduced last century, it was predominantly male. Not only were whites frightened that the 'lower races' might breed if coloured women entered but, as Saunders comments, those Pacific Island women who did enter, and whose menfolk provided the Kanaka labour in Queensland's sugar fields, were not themselves acceptable initially as indentured servants

> ...because their reproductive capacities could endanger the whole structure of an easily replaceable, fluid, servile labour force...

Yet, when employers required an expanding labour force for the cane fields this led the white masters to change their minds so that they reasoned:

> If field labour was 'nigger's work', then Island women could be allocated with impunity (Saunders, 1982:32).

Racism, like nationalism, comes in many different forms (Hall, 1978:26; Miles, 1982:101) and often race, nation and culture are conflated. What all varieties emphasise are both exclusion from the race, nation or culture and inclusion in the chosen 'we' group. Both exclusion and inclusion work differently for men and women.

During the late nineteenth century and in the period of the White Australia Policy it was often said of poor whites that they breed too fast, but on other occasions white women in general were portrayed as virtuous, rather stupid and in need of protection from the men of other races, particularly from the 'savage' Asiatics. Clergymen, politicians and journalists were all concerned. As the *Queensland Evangelical Standard* cried in 1876:

> What happiness can any poor foolish country woman of ours expect from uniting in marriage with a soft, pulpy, childish but passionate kanaka or the light, yellow-skinned mummy of the Celestial Empire? (quoted in Evans et al., 1975:262)

The media were not alone; from the 1880s politicians vigorously opposed miscegenation in parliamentary debates on restrictive legislation, and instances of Anglo-Asian births were condemned (Curthoys, 1958:98;

81

Markus, 1985:11,13). Some spokesmen even argued for an instinct against intermarriage 'which seeks to save us from an act fatal to us as a *species'* (quoted in Cronin, 1975:293). This so-called instinct however seems to have been sex-specific, located in women only, because on the frontier and elsewhere white men violated Aboriginal women who were deemed unworthy of protection. Even if unions between black and white were not violent, their issue was commonly designated 'half-caste', if not 'the worst of both worlds'.

Even in the twentieth century non-Europeans and Aboriginals were considered unfit as citizens of the democratic, white nation until the 1960s (Palfreeman, 1967). Aboriginal people were not even counted in the census until 1966. Some non-European men resided here but non-European women particularly were excluded during this period or, if permitted entry (as Indians were after 1919), the permission depended on satisfactory reports as to their husbands' or fathers' capacity to support them. Yet discriminatory state legislation often made this extremely difficult if not impossible for the men (de Lepervanche, 1984:60-69). In 1961 the number of overseas-born Chinese males in Australia was 11,287 compared with 3,545 females: the overseas-born Indian males numbered 2,683 compared with 367 females (Palfreeman, 1967:145-6).

Not surprisingly then, until very recently the Australian nation was perceived as a racially and culturally homogeneous community (Markus, 1985:11) and the fertility of white women was of prime importance to those men in power. Immigration schemes introduced white settlers, predominantly from the United Kingdom, to populate the land, and in one way or another the desire for a high white birthrate has long been a national priority (Gordon, 1975; Cass, 1983b:177). Women's reproductive capacities, their dependent status and their association with mothering have all been crucial in the ideological battles around the issues of race and nation.

If women did not play their part properly as breeders, the race and nation were in danger. Indeed, the potential for both race and nation of properly performed motherhood was enormous. As one authority put it early this century:

> Gaols, reformatories, policemen, all the paraphernalia of punishment that are supposed to be necessary to protect the world from the criminal might be scrapped and thrown into the limbo of mistaken opportunities, if only mothers would understand their duty and learn how to do it (quoted in Reiger, 1982:811).

Falling birthrates regularly upset our public spokesmen: as the rate in Australia fell from 38 per 1000 in 1870 to 27 per 1000 in 1900, alarm spread in government circles. Male explanations for the decline included the use of contraception by women, which allegedly contributed to 'race suicide'. A 1903 report by the Commonwealth Statistician noted that the limitation of family size was a selfish and decadent phenomenon (McQueen, 1978:60, Coghlan, 1903). In 1920 the New South Wales Minister for Public Health and Motherhood warned in parliament that throughout the world:

> ...the black races are breeding ten to one of the white races... The only way to alter the balance in favour of the white races is to ensure that the women who are prepared to do their duty should not be penalised... (NSW Parliamentary Debates 1920:4087, quoted in Cass, 1983a:68-9).

It is sobering to realise that the maternal mortality rate in Australia actually rose between 1910 and 1930. In the 1920s it accounted for one-sixth of deaths of married women in early and mid-adult life (Roe, 1983:10). Never mind, women's job was breeding the race and in 1938, when the nation celebrated the 150th anniversary of Phillip's landing, women as breeders were honoured in pageant and verse. One example from a poetry competition included the following:

> Ye girls of British race
> Famous for your beauty
> Breed fast in all your grace
> For this is your duty.
> As Anzac gave in war
> So daughters at your call
> Will quick respond the more
> To replace those that fall (quoted in McQueen 1978:158).

Since 1938 we have been through a few more wars and labour shortages: women have regularly been exhorted to breed but we eventually had to abandon the White Australia Policy and stop talking about race as we used to. It was bad for trade with our Pacific neighbours. During World War II, however, womens duty temporarily broadened beyond breeding: they were expected to 'man' the factories for warwork. Afterwards they were encouraged to return to the home and breed while immigrants from the United Kingdom and northern Europe arrived to augment our numbers.

After the war, the stress on the assimilation of these newcomers to the 'Australian Way of Life' in government policy contradicted notions of racial or ethnic separateness and emphasised instead Anglo-conformism as a superior way of life. Under this policy other peoples' race, ethnicity and/ or culture, including the Aboriginals', were potentially adaptable in the interests of national unity. Then in 1973, with the first Labor government in 23 years, policy on immigration changed and since then it has stressed multiculturalism, family reunion and the celebration of diverse ethnicities. We had by then many non-British settlers and had even begun to introduce some Asians. Provided they were technically or professionally qualified, i.e. of relatively high status, Asian male principals (as they are called) were accepted with their dependent wives and children from the late 1960s (Rivett, 1975).

With multiculturalism the accent fell on 'the family of the nation' (Grassby, 1973): indeed the family rather than the race became the heart of our national way of life. But the change from assimilation to multiculturalism accompanied another fall in the birthrate during the 1970s. National population enquiries followed and women were again publicly urged to breed (Cass, 1983b:177, 181). Their failure to do so was even cited as a cause for the 1970s recession (Dowse, 1983:219), and in 1977 the Anglican Archbishop of Sydney criticised both State and Federal Governments for funding Women's Health and Rape Crises Centres, saying that they 'disturb and destroy the inherited moral standards and values of our nation' and actively promote 'drastic change in normal human relationships' (SMH, 5 October 1977). 'Normal human relationships' mean women at home breeding. During the 1979 Abortion Debate in Federal Parliament the Minister for Health was reported as deploring the prevalence of abortion and the increased use of contraception. Both, he said, had upset planning projections and it would require a massive immigration programme to effect a population increase. Another MP concluded that Australia was on the path to self-genocide (SMH, 23 March 1979). Those women who did go out to work found (and still find) that women in general earn lower average wages than men and that grossly inadequate childcare facilities disadvantage them (Power et al., 1984).

The plurality of the nation's component ethnic groups today are not equal in status, and the workforce is segmented by ethnic origin and gender (Collins, 1984). Compared with Anglophone white males, southern European immigrants, for example, tend to fill the lower paid, less secure jobs, and immigrant women are particularly disadvantaged in this respect (Bottomly, 1984a; Martin, 1984; Collins, 1984). In addition, ethnic politics as well as national affairs remain in the hands of men (Jacubowicz, 1984).

Persons from all ethnic groups are entitled to apply for family reunions, but it is common for males to introduce dependent kin; and although women in general are enjoined to breed it would seem that even as breeders some women are more favoured than others. The less privileged have been targets for doses of the drug Depo Provera, which prevents conception, despite the fact that the Australian Drug Evaluation Committee in 1977 ruled that it cannot be promoted as a contraceptive: its use may only occur on a trial or 'investigational' basis if administered to a patient on the basis of her 'informed' consent (Fraser and Weisberg, 1981). It is not known how many women are using the drug or how many have been informed of its potential risks, but reports have surfaced concerning its use on illiterate women who allegedly 'could not remember to take a pill every night', on Aboriginal and some immigrant women (*Right to Choose,* No. 22 1981:5; Melbourne *Age,* 27 March 1981; *SMH*, 28 February 1981; Sydney *Sun*, 17 November 1975; *National Times,* 15-21 March 22-28 March 1981; Bottomley, 1984b).

Other forms of cultural constraints potentially affect all women. In Australia, as in Britain and Europe, racist and sexist ideologies have flourished with the post-war introduction of immigrant labour into many of the underprivileged jobs, and more recently as many locals and immigrants have become unemployed (Collins, 1975; 1984:21-24). As recession deepened in the West, the divisions between the many cultures and the so-called races or ethnic groups have been ever more clearly etched on the public mind by a new kind of argument that avoids mention of colour or race altogether, and which, unlike old-fashioned racism, does not mention inferior or superior endowments either. This new argument is part of an attempt to reconstitute a commonsense in which cultural difference *is* recognised but in which all peoples allegedly share a *common* human nature which 'naturally' inclines us to nepotism and to exclude whoever is alien to our way of life (Barker, 1981:25). This common sense sanctions ethnocentrism and provides what Barker calls the 'new racism' (1981). This common sense with its common human nature also constructs woman as breeder, within the family: as one MP in Britain put it:

> It is part of the British way of life for the father to provide a home for the family, and it is the same in India... There is no rational argument in favour of saying that a wife in another country should be in a position to provide a home for her husband and children. It is contrary to all commonsense, human nature, and the way of life of both Britain and the subcontinent (Stanbrook, Hansard p.1052 quoted in Barker, 1981:23).

This common human nature not only informs common sense, it has also been legitimated by sociobiology. As the founder of this so-called science argues, 'Nationalism and racism... are the culturally nurtured outgrowths of simple tribalism' (Wilson, 1978:92). And 'simple tribalism', according to the sociobiologists' theory of kin selection, is rooted in family relationships. As van den Berghe expresses it: 'all known human societies are organised on the basis of kinship and marriage, forming relatively stable reproductive units called families and exhibiting preferential behaviour towards relatives' (1981:21).   •

Women's subordination in the domestic world of family is then explained by the sociobiologists' theory of parental investment; Trivers' version goes as follows;

85

...a copulation costing the male virtually nothing may trigger a nine-month investment by the female... followed... by a fifteen-year investment in the offspring... Although the male may often contribute parental care during this period, he need not necessarily do so. After a nine-month pregnancy, a female is more or less free to terminate her investment at any moment but doing so wastes her investment up until then. Given the initial imbalance in investment the male may maximise his chances of leaving surviving offspring by copulating and abandoning many females, some of whom, alone or with the aid of others, will raise his offspring (1978:62).

Nowhere does Trivers suggest that a crucial difference exists between bearing and rearing children. His scenario simply reproduces our stereotyped sex roles.

In Australia a version of this new commonsense, or new racism, has its most articulate spokesman in Geoffrey Blainey. He has not explicitly invoked sociobiology to support his views but he has clearly stated his value orientation which coincides in many ways with those who find sociobiology so attractive. For instance, in criticising present government immigration policy with respect to Asian entry, he says 'a family-reunion scheme is overwhelmingly a racial-reunion scheme' (1984:98), whereas the 'typical nation practises discrimination against migrants, for the sake of national unity' (1984:52). If Australia continued to treat all peoples of the world as equally eligible as immigrants, he argues, and the Asian percentage became the dominant stream, the 'Asian and Third World domination of the migrant lists would be self generating, and Australia would eventually become an Asian nation' (1984:119). Blainey complains that recent Australian governments have cut 'the crimson threads' of kinship with Britain and thereby disowned our past (1984:159), and now the 'desire to turn Australia into a new nation, a nation of all nations... contradicts the increasing sense of national pride that has become so vivid since the Whitlam era' (1984:153).

Here, of course, Blainey conflates race with nation and culture, and, like the sociobiologists, 'racial' homogeneity with social cohesion. He frankly admits to white ancestry from the British Isles and to a clear preference for 'our kind of society and most of its ruling values' (1984:17). These ruling values still include privileges for Anglo conformity and a subordinate status for women, otherwise we would have no need for anti-discrimination legislation.

Yet, Blainey faces a particular problem not shared by those who hold similar views in the UK. There, the new racism wants to exclude blacks and Asians from a country that has been white for thousands of years, and it includes in the definition of human nature an instinct to defend a home territory. As Enoch Powell proclaimed;

> An instinct to preserve an identity and defend a territory is one of the deepest and strongest implanted in mankind... (Powell on BBC 1, 9 June, 1969, quoted in Barker, 1981:22).

In Australia, the whites by comparison are the recent invaders. Blainey's argument for maintaining the crimson thread of British kinship has to justify white conquest over the Aboriginal people, which he does implicitly in his histories by lauding the white (male) pioneers with their sweat, grit and ingenuity (1984:159), compared with the less developed nomads who initially inhabited the place less than 200 years ago (cf. Blainey in *Triumph of the Nomads* 1(1975); and cf. Reynolds, 1985). The white pioneers who penetrated the interior do not include women, and here Blainey's view of the Australian identity conforms to other (male) depictions of the national character as white, male and British (cf. Aveling, 1985:92).

Modern multiculturalism has not done much more for women either. Under 'White Australia' women were the rather stupid, passive breeders of the white race; in today's multicultural society pressures remain on women to stay in or return to the family, to reproduce and nurture. Although many white Anglo and European women resist these pressures, for some immigrant women resistance is not so easy. As Humphreys explains for Lebanese women;

> The institutional arrangements which have traditionally diminished the prerogatives of husbands and transferred these to courts and judges throughout the Middle East are largely absent in immigrant Muslim communities... even the legal importance of religious... opinion issued by learned judges and *muftis*, which has been greatly restricted as a result of law reform in the Middle East, is reasserted in these immigrant communities (1984:195).

From my own experience, I have heard a Sikh male elder explain why young Sikh women cannot have the same freedom as young men to mix with locals as Australians do: Women, he said, 'tarnish more easily'.

In examining the cultural construction of race, then, we need to examine thoroughly the associated notions of nation and national identity and their interrelationship with gender difference and inequality. As the spotlight shines upon the family as *the* reproductive unit both in political rhetoric and sociobiological discourse, women's central position as breeder locates us at the point of transmission of cultural values and of cultural difference. This has implications for women that are worth exploring much further if we wish to assert and maintain our autonomy and challenge patriarchal conceptions of ourselves and others.

References

Anderson, B. (1983) *Imagined Communities,* London, Verso.

Aveling, M. (1985) 'Blainey and Being Australian', in A. Markus and M.C. Ricklefs (eds): *Surrender Australia?* Sydney, Allen and Unwin.

Barker, M. (1981) *The New Racism,* London, Junction Books.

Blainey, G. (1984) *All For Australia,* Sydney, Methuen Haynes.

Bottomley, G. (1984a) 'Women on the move: migration and feminism' in G. Bottomley and M. de Lepervanche (eds): *Ethnicity, Class and Gender in Australia.* Sydney, Allen and Unwin, pp.98-108.

Bottomley, G. (1984b) 'Mediterranean Women in Australia: An Overview'. Paper presented at a Symposium of Mediterranean Women's Organisations, Delphi, Greece, 5-8 April.

Cass, B. (1983a) 'Redistribution to Children and to Mothers; a history of Child Endowment and Family Allowances' in C.V. Baldock and B. Cass (eds) *Women, Social Welfare and the State,* Sydney, Allen & Unwin, pp.54-84.

Cass, B. (1983b) 'Population Policies and Family Policies: State Construction of Domestic Life' in C.V. Baldock and B. Cass (eds) *Women, Social Welfare and the State,* Sydney, Allen and Unwin, pp.164-185.

Coghlan, T.A. (1903) *The Decline in the Birth Rate of New South Wales.* Sydney, Government Printer.

Collins, J. (1975) 'The Political Economy of Post-War Immigration' in E.L. Wheelwright and K. Buckley (eds): *Essays in the Political Economy of Australian Capitalism.* Vol. 1. Sydney, ANZ Book Co., pp.105-129.

Collins, J. (1984) 'Immigration and Class: the Australian Ex perience' in G. Bottomley and M. de Lepervanche (eds): *Ethnicity, Class and Gender in Australia.* Sydney, Allen & Unwin, pp.1-27.

Cronin, K. (1975) 'The Yellow Agony', in R. Evans et.al., (eds) *Exclusion, Exploitation and Extermination,* Sydney, ANZ Book Co.

Curthoys, A. (1975) 'Towards a Feminist Labour History' in A. Curthoys et.al., (eds): *Women at Work,* Canberra, Australian Society for the Study of Labour History.

Curthoys, A. (1985) 'Racism and Class in the Nineteenth-Century Immigration Debate' in A. Markus and M.C. Ricklefs (eds): *Surrender Australia?* Sydney, Allen & Unwin.

Dowse, S. (1983) 'The Women's Movement's Fandango with the State: the Movement's Role in Public Policy Since 1972.' In C.V. Baldock and B. Cass (eds) *Women, Social Welfare and the State.* Sydney, Allen & Unwin, pp.201-222.

Evans, R. et.al. (1975) *Exclusion, Exploitation and Extermination; Race Relations in Colonial Queensland.* Sydney, ANZ Book Co.

Fraser, I.S., and Weisberg, E. (1981) 'A Comprehensive Review of Injectable Contraception with Special Emphasis on Depot Medroxyprogesterone Acetate', *Medical Journal of Australia,* Vol. 1., No. 1, 24 January, Special Supplement.

Gordon, L. (1975) 'Race Suicide and the Feminist Response', in *Hecate,* Vol. 1, No. 2, pp.40-50.

Grassby, A.J. (1973) 'A Multi-Cultural Society for the Future.' Immigration Reference Paper, Department of Immigration, Canberra, AGPS.

Hall, S. (1978) 'Racism and Reaction', in *Five Views of Multi-Racial Britain.* London Commission for Racial Equality.

Humphrey, M. (1984) 'Religion, Law and Family Disputes in a Lebanese Muslim Community in Sydney', in G. Bottomley and M. de Lepervanche (eds): *Ethnicity, Class and Gender in Australia*. Sydney, Allen & Unwin, pp.183-198.

Jakubowicz, A. (1984) 'Ethnicity, Multiculturalism and Neo-Conservatism' in G. Bottomley and M. de Lepervanche (eds): *Ethnicity, Class and Gender in Australia*, Sydney, Allen & Unwin, pp.28-48.

de Lepervanche, M. (1984) *Indians in a White Australia*. Sydney, Allen & Unwin.

McQueen, H. (1978) *Social Sketches of Australia 1888-1975*. Harmondsworth, Penguin.

Markus, A. (1985) '1984 or 1901? Immigration and Some "lessons" of Australian History', in A. Markus and M.C. Ricklefs (eds): *Surrender Australia?* Sydney, Allen & Unwin.

Markus, A., and Ricklefs, M.C. (eds) (1985) *Surrender Australia? Essays in the Study and Uses of History*. Sydney, Allen & Unwin.

Martin, J. (1984) 'Non-English Speaking Women: Production and Social Reproduction', in G. Bottomley and M. de Lepervanche (eds): *Ethnicity, Class and Gender in Australia*. Sydney, Allen & Unwin, pp.109-122.

Miles, R. (1982) *Racism and Migrant Labour*. London, Routledge & Kegan Paul.

Palfreeman, A.C. (1967) *The Administration of the White Australia Policy*. Melbourne University Press.

Power, M. et.al. (1984) 'Writing Women Out of the Economy'. Paper presented to From Margin to Mainstream: A National Conference About Women and Employment. Melbourne, 16 October.

Reiger, K. (1982) 'Women's Labour Redefined: Childbearing and Rearing Advice in Australia 1880-1930s, in M. Bevege et.al. (eds) *Worth Her Salt; Women at Work in Australia*. Sydney, Hale & Iremonger, pp.72-83.

Reynolds, H. (1985) 'Blainey and Aboriginal History', in A. Markus and M.C. Ricklefs (eds) *Surrender Australia?*, Sydney, Allen & Unwin.

Rivett, K. (1975) *Australia and the Non-White Migrant*. Melbourne University Press.

Roe, J. (1975) 'Social Policy and the Permanent Poor' in E.L. Wheelwright and K. Buckley (eds) *Essays in the Political Economy of Australian Capitalism* Vol. I, Sydney, ANZ Book Co., pp.130-152.

Roe, J. (1983) 'The End is Where We Start From: Women and Welfare Since 1901' in C.V. Baldock and B. Cass (eds) *Women, Social Welfare and the State*. Sydney, Allen & Unwin, pp.1-19.

Saunders, K. (1982) 'Pacific Islander Women in Queensland: 1863-1907' in M. Bevege et.al. (eds) *Worth Her Salt*. Sydney, Hale & Iremonger, pp.16-32.

Trivers, R. (1978) 'Parental Investment and Sexual Selection' in T.H. Clutton-Brock and P.H. Harvey (eds) *Readings in Sociobiology*, San Francisco, W.H. Freeman.

van den Berghe, P. (1981) *The Ethnic Phenomenon*. New York, Elsevier.

Wilson, E.O. (1978) *On Human Nature,* Harvard University Press.

The Cultural Deconstruction of Racism: Education and Multiculturalism

Mary Kalantzis

In this paper I examine attempts at the deconstruction of racism in the contemporary Australian context, particularly in the fields of education and multicultural policy and practice. By this, I mean deconstruction not only in terms of the epistemological explanation of racism and multiculturalism in schools, but also the practical imperatives arising from analysis, which include an attempt to dismantle racism. What I am referring to then is a dual analytical and interventionist project which is struggling to make its mark.

I choose the areas of multiculturalism and education for two reasons. First, schooling in Australia is a compulsory, universal experience and therefore an important site for examination, both as the reflection and reflector of processes of socialisation. Second, the questions of so-called 'race' and 'race relations' as introduced through multiculturalism, although misshapen and problematic, have made their most widespread inroads into education, albeit often only obliquely through the concepts of culture and ethnicity.

A critique of multiculturalism is crucial to any exercise in the deconstruction of racism because multiculturalism begins by asking some very important questions - What is Australian society like? What could it be like? Given Australia's history, the response to these questions, both in terms of analysis and possible intervention, implicates the issue of racism.

But aside from this, and perhaps more importantly, the framework within which the multicultural movement worked by and large is indicative of a more general phenomenon in the dynamic of modern industrial societies which have had to deal with, mask and/ or transform the history of racist practices and ideology. The nation state of advanced industrial society can no longer draw its identity from a single homogeneous ethnic group. It does, as its rhetoric says, have to create cohesion out of diversity, but to do this it has to make the diverse groups appear equal. Multiculturalism springs from this new imperative. It addresses the traditional question of race in a new guise through the politics of difference buttressed by a keenly developed notion of the individual and of plurality (cf. Barker, 1981).

But it still has history to contend with. Briefly, Australia has had a continuous history of racism both in terms of processes that have structured social life, such that certain groups of people have been disadvantaged, and which have produced prejudices that are linked directly or indirectly to such processes. In terms of the pre-existing Aboriginal settlement, the establishment of western society and, later, industrialism in Australia has involved systematic and conscious violence that is now so well documented (cf. Rowley, 1970; Reynolds, 1981). That many Australians choose to dismiss or ignore the origins of their own everyday life forms in Australia shows that this historical act of racism is, in an important sense, continuous and still incomplete.

In the process of European settlement there emerged a second history of racism, namely, against certain immigrants who brought their own patterns of solidarity with them and who were distinguishably 'different', such as the Irish and the Chinese in the nineteenth century and the post-war non-Anglophone migrants and refugees of the twentieth century. However, it was not difference that fashioned racism so much as the structural location of each new group, insofar as it appeared to threaten organised labour and the order of those already established (cf. Collins, 1975; de Lepervanche, 1975).

On the other side of this coin, racism has been used by post-war governments to sell their immigration programs to the Australian people. Immigration, according to the rhetoric, need not threaten Australian society because only those who could be readily, and relatively easily, assimilated would be brought in. Into the 1960s, there was an implicit argument embodied in the White Australia Policy that Europeans who were like us would create jobs and improve living standards, but Asians would have a deleterious effect because they were unlike us. People were thus actively consoled about migration through ideological arguments along racist lines. Nor has racism been the exclusive preserve of longer-established Australians. Newer migrants in some circumstances bring their own forms of racism, born of entirely different historic circumstances from those in Australia.

Yet very contradictorily, openness and plurality sit beside these histories of racism. Modern industrial societies and the international migration of labour throw people of different backgrounds together although there are no natural reasons why people should be racist. Labour force segmentation, however, is an integral part of the functioning of modern industrial societies, and ethnic segmentation is a part of this in Australia today, thus

91

providing the structural bases for a new racism. The liberalising, equalising dynamic of modern industrial society in some respects therefore confronts the structural underpinnings of racism (cf. Collins, 1984).

It is this history that multiculturalism has had to address and rework. It does so in two ways: one by description and the other by prescription. The description is a truism. There are people in Australia of many different so-called 'racial', cultural or ethnic backgrounds. The function of the energy expended in this description is to contribute information that will allow the servicing of this diversity. This has been particulary important given that, for a while from the late 1960s, many migrants were leaving to go back home, thus Australia was losing on their social cost. Another critical aspect of this description is its effect on the other prong of multiculturalism - its prescription for Australian society. But prescription is not a simple matter. The description and declaration of Australia as a Multicultural Society is part of the strategy for forging a new national identity, of promoting some pleasant state of harmony between the various groupings. As such it indicates two things.

First, the new nation does not need a single 'ethnic' or 'racial' descriptor. The rallying symbols could well be a famous yacht, a brand of coffee or a soft drink jingle. A certain diversity at the level of skin colour, language, customs and so on, is characteristic of all modern industrial societies, given their histories of interaction with indigenous peoples, labour migration and their relations with a world market. Second, the fact that there is a need for such prescription necessarily implies that things are not so pleasant. The superficial pleasant diversity has embedded within it another diversity: that of inequality (cf. Bottomley and de Lepervanche, 1984).

But there is tension in the prescriptive task of multiculturalism. Something that has been as integral and as functional as racism, so long an element in Australian history, cannot be deconstructed so easily. And there have been very few within the social arenas using the term multiculturalism, either as a policy or servicing device, who have been prepared to tackle seriously what has been 'unpleasant' in the construction of our newly professed plurality. The exceptions would be some of the Aboriginal people.

Multiculturalism only declares difference by counting the numbers and superficially describing the features of the different 'racial', ethnic or cultural groupings. Overwhelmingly, the strategy employed for intervention in an attempt to overcome 'unpleasantness' is to soften the heart. The keywords in the rhetoric have been 'attitudes', 'self-esteem', 'tolerance', 'respect', 'understanding' and 'sensitisation'. The main goal has been to encourage people to feel good about difference. After all, modern industrial societies simply have to function smoothly. This condition just happens to have involved, along the way, the usurpation of the structural basis for the reproduction of life of the indigenous people and the massive migration of cheap labour from distant and unevenly developed parts of the world. Yet, these events are silences in the pleasant discourse of multiculturalism.

To achieve this goal of smooth functioning, multiculturalism in Australia has had to attempt three things. First it has had to respond to the demands of those indigenous people who survived, so as to appear to transform the first major racist moment in Australian history. Second, it has needed to break long-standing ideologies of parochialism and racial prejudice in the dominant so-called anglo-Australian population. And third, it has curiously had to support traditionalism for 'ethnics' and indigenous people in the search for something that appears to demonstrate their cultural autonomy and social equality.

These tasks create a problem which in part is resolved by defining what can be 'multi' in Australia in a very narrow way: essentially all those things that are private and conducted in spare time. If what defines people's identity is something they do in their spare time, unique to them as individuals, and if all these things are held to be equal - colour of skin, food, music, religion and so on - deep practices of racism and other structural inequalities are masked. The fact that non-English speaking people are disproportionally represented at the bottom of the social pile and that many indigenous people do not figure in the pile at all, can be ignored.

The ethnic or cultural revival that is supposed to be part of multiculturalism is not anti-racist in any significant way because it refers predominantly to difference only at the level of cultural phenomena. In fact, it could be said that its effect has been mainly to displace the issue of racism thereby masking its history.

This is precisely what is happening in schools. The interpretation of culture and ethnicity mainly at the level of cultural phenomena has contributed to an understanding of difference that masks inequality, that ignores the pedagogical imperatives of modern industrial societies and that provides an inadequate social analysis. In consequence, despite its intentions, multiculturalism can and does end up being racist. Singing and dancing on the dole queue in your community language, happy to be ethnic, does not dismantle racism.

Of course, the task of dismantling racism cannot be put solely at the feet of education. But a focus on education does provide a good case study of the requirements of deconstruction both at the level of analysis and intervention. If we take New South Wales as an example, the empirical evidence bears out the contradictory nature of multicultural education as it is

93

presently practised and reveals the limitations of its interventions in contributing to the dismantling of racism.

At the level of policy, the rhetoric is full of phrases like 'diversity with cohesion' and it demands that 'multiculturalism' be viewed as a 'positive' term. So, right from the start, 'negative' things like 'racism', as a process that produced the plurality as an effect, are disallowed. In 1983-84 for example, the Multicultural Education Co-ordinating Committee of New South Wales allocated 50% of its 1.5 million dollars annual budget to community languages, 25% to ethnic liaison officers, 10% to Aboriginal education and 15% to socio-cultural projects. In the socio-cultural category, the average grant was for about $2,000 and went towards projects with titles like 'Intercultural Understanding', 'Multicultural History of Batlow', 'Finger-painting - a multicultural experience' (That received $8,000) and 'Who is an Australian?'. Understanding through exposure to difference and the promotion of self-esteem through the school's recognition and teaching of parents' language are the main emphases.

The other major prong of funding, to English as a Second Language (ESL) teaching, is so poorly funded and supported in comparison to the needs, that it often does not prepare children beyond survival English (Campbell, 1984: Campbell and McMeniman, 1985). So its capacity to counter-balance the effects of structural racism is limited. At the teacher training level, one example of this limited intervention is a course called 'Culture Contact in the Classroom'. Its seminars include 'Finding out about other Cultures', Ethnicity and Identity', 'Ethnic Institutions in Australia' and 'Culture Bias'.

The sites for action signalled in these examples have of course made spaces for some people and some projects that do tackle racism head on. The scene is not entirely bleak. But my argument is that positive measures are minimal because the analysis that informs intervention disallows a systematic and rigorous understanding of racism.

Issues pertaining to structural racism, such as underachievement at school, the need for alternative credentialling for indigenous people and those of non-English speaking background, inadequacies of access in the transition from school to work, the traumas of settlement and serious cultural conflict, are all sidestepped. The fact that some people consider Australian Aborigines in their daily interactions today as inferior does not itself create their inequality. Their current position can only really be understood in terms of the structural effects of racism in Australian history. Telling Aboriginal people that their traditional practices and products are still important, putting their visual images into galleries, does not provide either the basis for reproducing their culture as something other than 'commodities' or 'art' (neither of which they were in traditional gathering and

94

hunting life), nor does it equip them for contemporary self-determination.

There is a real fear and reluctance in schools to address these issues of racism; their displacement into happy philosophies of 'difference' exacerbates this tendency. There exists in schools a general tendency to believe that children only experience racism as attitudes and therefore a teacher can work at the problem simply at this level. Thus schools typically assert either that racism is not too much of a problem in Australia or, if it is a problem, then it is just a matter of changing one's heart. Within this framework, racism becomes a moral lapse that can be rectified by imbibing sentiments like 'everyone is beautiful in their own way, even if they are different from me' or, 'all differences are of equal value and should be respected'. In this model, racism is viewed as an accident of individual pathology which is rectifiable by therapy.

When, on one piece of research, we asked children in schools what it is like living in a society like Australia with people from different backgrounds, their answers included many comments such as the following: 'My mum can't read or write and can't help me with my homework.' 'My dad works like a kid in the factory of the cakes.' 'It feels like you are being invaded.' 'We will have to widen our industries.' 'We will need more graveyards.' 'I'm not allowed to have Australian friends.' 'I know I'll be on the dole.' The children themselves consistently raised problems that could not be resolved simply by the learning of their own community languages or those of others. Self-esteem and integrity comes with the possibility of full social participation, not with being patted on the head for being 'ethnic' or 'different' (Kalantzis and Cope, 1981).

In public debate multiculturalism has contested meanings. Part of this contest involves redefining the term so that its stated goals can be realised. A diverse society of equals is surely a worthy aim. A non-racist society, even if not of equals, is another worthy goal. There is also an important task in removing from the process of social segmentation those explanations of inequality that rely on the 'natural', as racism does. That is, an analysis of cultural plurality in Australia that recognises the historic role of racism in fashioning social relations between those elements that constitute diversity would prescribe something quite different from the current predominant practices of multiculturalism.

Very briefly, in the area of schooling, this prescription would involve affirmative action that aimed to remove the structures of inequality at the level of the whole school. It would mean at the compulsory levels of schooling a core curriculum that had equal outcomes as a goal. The push to diversified, school-based curricula that is now in full swing in New South Wales would not be used, as they minimise the life chances of children of non-English speaking backgrounds by masking their needs. The alternative I suggest could make possible creative, intensive responses to redress the effects of structural inequality (Kalantzis and Cope, 1985). For instance, the process of language learning would not be one that drew mainly upon the rationale of building self-esteem through respect for cultural difference, but would consider language as a tool for communication, action, power and self-determination (Kalantzis and Cope, 1986).

Teacher training would not rely on 'finding out about other cultures'. The emphasis would be more on the pedagogical imperatives of modern industrial societies as they relate to all people irrespective of their backgrounds, and there would be an emphasis on the acquisition of skills that make genuine cultural choices possible. This would involve every teacher in language training across all disciplines.

With respect to materials and curriculum, the task is not simply to remove stereotyping and widen ethnic representation, but to develop coherent and sustained mainstream programs and resources that enable all students to understand the processes of their cultural construction. To that end, it is important that in Australia at the moment the current dichotomy between curriculum process and curriculum content is resolved. It needs to be recognised that there is a specific and necessary content to an anti-racist curriculum.

The Social Literacy Project provides an example of an alternative model. It is a materials development project funded by the Multicultural Education Co-ordinating Committee of New South Wales, initially by accident, and against some conventional curriculum and multicultural wisdoms. It consists of social science materials for upper primary and lower secondary students. Its strategy is to argue to the head rather than the heart on issues of racism. Children, through a series of content inputs, are placed in experiences that facilitate the acquiring of conceptual tools for social analysis. The goal is the acquisition of knowledge and the examination of life practices that will inform them of the processes involved in becoming an 'ethnic', 'a white', 'a female', and so on. The outcome to which the program aspires is confident, effective, social participation and not the affective goal of absorbing tolerance by osmosis through exposure to difference.

For example, an input in the primary materials on Robinson Crusoe as the great individual who survived on his own by his natural skills, is the requirement to rethink this story to discover that Robinson did not survive on that island on his own. His 'natural' skills involved social products: a gun, a bible, a language and so on, all products constructed by many others in the culture in which he had been an active memeber. And such was the effect of his socialisation that when he met Man Friday, he presumed he had no faith, no language, no skills and so Robinson proceeded not only to dominate his homeland but to transform Friday into a 'human', 'cultured' construct. The children engage in the activity as fun. The process is discovery learning. But the experience is structured to ensure examination of the concepts of sociality, the individual, culture as learnt, ethnicity and so on.

So far as content is concerned, the starting point for the Social Literacy materials are points of unity in the human experience: the need to satisfy basic human needs, be they material, spiritual or emotional. Difference is explored as historically and socially constructed. The approach is an holistic one, as opposed to a one-sided stress on phenomenal difference as in 'ethnic studies'. For example, it could be said that Australia is a plural society because you can go to a shop and buy Lebanese bread, white (Australian) sliced bread and Swiss bread. An activity associated with the discovery of this fact could be a school excursion to a Sydney suburb during which students could observe, record, classify and report on the differences they encountered in the shops on the main street.

The Social Literacy Project approaches its task in another way. For, although it is true that bread is an example of cultural diversity in Australia, this exists only at a certain level, because the way that Lebanese bread (made in factories, packed into plastic bags, and sold in shops) is produced and consumed is exactly the same as that for white sliced or Swiss bread. What is more important than dwelling on the phenomenon of difference is the structure of social relations associated with the apparent differences. At the level of everyday life, where Lebanese bread is part of a culture of take-away food, for example, the non-plurality is more profound than the plurality.

In terms of general outcomes, the Social Literacy materials stress the acquisition of skills in the form of a language that empowers children and makes active self-creation possible. By contrast, many of the efforts currently made in schools of high migrant density are tending to involve a slippage in what is offered to their students. Schools often go overboard trying to make kids feel good about being different. The structural bases of those differences are not examined.

Materials like those developed by the Social Literacy Project are an important part of anti-racist strategies in schools because they not only serve the immediate needs of the teachers wishing to respond to the issues but they also serve the purpose of educating the educators in a sensitive and confused field. Such materials have to be aimed at all children in the first instance

97

and incorporate skills as well as analysis (Kalantzis and Cope 1981, 1985; Kalantzis et.al., 1986).

But none of the strategies mentioned above can work on their own. Yet, in each case they can become catalysts for a broader critical education and for social action. The question of racism, most importantly, should not be viewed as one of psychology or moral lapse. Nor should anti-racist education become submerged in the celebration of diversity.

References

Barker, M. (1981) *The New Racism* London, Junction Books.
Bottomley, G. and de Lepervanche, M. (eds) (1984) *Ethnicity, Class and Gender in Australia* Sydney, Allen & Unwin.
Campbell, W.J. et.al. (1984) 'A Review of the Commonwealth English as a Second Language (ESL) Programme' Canberra, AGPS.
Campbell, W.J., and McMeniman, M.M. (1985) 'Bridging the Language Gap: Ideals and Realities Pertaining to Learning English as a Second Language' Canberra, AGPS.
Collins, J. (1984) 'Immigration and Class: the Australian Experience' in G. Bottomley and M. de Lepervanche (eds) *Ethnicity, Class and Gender in Australia* Sydney, Allen & Unwin.
Kalantzis, M. and Cope, B. (1981) *Just Spaghetti and Polka? An Introduction to Australian Multicultural Education* Sydney, Social Literacy
Kalantzis, M., and Cope, B. (1985) 'Pluralism and Equitability: Multicultural Curriculum Strategies for Schools' Canberra, National Advisory Co-ordinating Committee on Multicultural Education.
Kalantzis, M. et.al., *The Language Question; The Maintenance of Language Other than English* 2 vols. Canberra, AGPS.
Reynolds, H. (1981) *The Other Side of the Frontier* Townsville, History Department, James Cook University.
Rowley, C.D. (1970) *The Destruction of Aboriginal Society* Vol. 1 Canberra, ANU Press.

Cio-Cio San: Object Butterfly

Mira Crouch

Madam Butterfly is Puccini's best known and, according to some commentators, most hackneyed work (cf. Drummond, 1980; Kerman, 1956). Such an evaluation is not inconsistent with the opera's popularity; quite the opposite may in fact be the case. Fortunately the parameters of this discussion allow us to eschew consideration of arguments regarding the aesthetic merits of the opera. Its popularity on the other hand certainly precipitates, for a social scientist, the search for its social meaning which, apart from its musico/ dramatic worth (questionable or otherwise), can be assumed to constitute at least part of the basis of its appeal. It is the contention of this paper that images of both gender and race are evoked by the main figure of the opera, Cio-Cio San (Madam Butterfly herself), and that it is the power of those images with all their connotations, brought forth by the dynamics of the music, that impresses and draws the opera's audiences.

The object of the present discussion, then, is a hermeneutic reconstruction of the dramatic and musical presentation of Butterfly. The hermeneutic process is a self-conscious engagement with the objects of perception in such a way as to transform them into personal constructs, to be relocated in the original context with the additional meaning taken into account. The image of Butterfly in a kimono singing her heart out, to us of another race, is a dynamic conception the sight and sound of which carry more significance, as communicative events, than is required by their formal relationships within the work as a whole. It is this significance towards which the hermeneutic effort here is directed.

Opera can be defined as 'staged drama unfolding integrally in words and music' (Donnington, 1981:20). Therefore the analysis of any such work cannot be restricted to the plot and the characterisations, as they unfold in the libretto (as well as through the specificities of any particular production). We must also consider the music, its integral part in the opera as a constituted 'ideal object' (Schutz, 1976) of perception and, taking the foregoing Schutzian account of music further, its effect on the 'real object' of a particular performance. This 'real object' (of our perception, as in the case of the 'ideal object') is constructed in action by both performers and audience in a web of shared as well as personal attitudes, beliefs, feelings and judgements. It is not argued here that this web is constitutive of the work as such; there is, after all, its existence as an 'ideal object' in the above sense, and, in addition, there is also a material aspect of any actual performance which takes place within the distinct boundaries of a specific spatial arrangement and consists, in that material sense of the sounds and the bodies which produce them (cf. Supicic, 1970). It is suggested, however, that this web constitutes, interactively and dynamically, the social meaning of opera which social science (as distinct from musicology, say) can seek to elucidate.

The dimming of the auditorium lights and the brackets of the proscenium symbolises the way in which the audience and, in a somewhat different manner, the performers suspend belief in their everyday common-sense knowledge of the world and enter the world of 'special time and place' (cf. Skadra, 1979) created on the stage and in the orchestra pit. Indeed, it is largely under the auspices of the music that this state of *epoche*, as it were, is accomplished. Under the influence of music, an 'island experience' arises out of everyday life (cf. Schutz, 1964); it is surrounded by, and simultaneously separated from, the life-world. The acts of daily existence are set aside, as is the concern with its objects and the attention is diverted to another plane of consciousness (cf. Schutz, 1978). It is the music that makes us apprehend opera as something more than the telling of a story. Fuelled and forged by sound, the images so created are capable of resonating at a deeply felt level, with associations freed from the evaluative framework of the common-sense understanding of the world. Yet in this process ubiquitous everyday experience is reached and illuminated.

It may be that the music makes repetition not only tolerable but desirable. Most opera attenders listen and go to opera performances frequently, hearing the same works a number of times. Perhaps it is the case that the bourgeois social milieu fosters such behaviour, which Adorno views critically as 'fetishism', suggesting that 'opera offers a paradigm... that is incessantly consumed' (Adorno, 1976'81) by those who have been designated as opera audiences by the structures of capitalist society. Undoubtedly there is a host of extrinsic factors which are involved in opera-going as social action; their consideration, however, is tangential to the present discussion. What is relevant here is the repetition, insofar as it means the audience of an opera, on the whole, knows the story the opera tells and can anticipate its musical sequences. Each moment of every performance takes place in full awareness of the total pattern of the work. This does not diminish the aesthetic and dramatic effects - on the contrary, it enhances them by enriching the perception with meaningful expectations. In this experience the music is the strongest integrating factor as it addresses the senses in a most immediate and imperative fashion. There is a dynamic relationship between this pressing immediacy and its embeddedness in the process of the inevitable unfolding of an already known pattern - and that relationship enables us, the opera audience, to cast off the syntagmatic chains which normally bind us to a plot in ordinary linear time. We are freed to explore, on the wings of song, the paradigm before us.

Thus it can be said, without fear of contradiction, that in such a frame of mind we can see the ultimate statement concerning the central character of *Madam Butterfly,* Cio-Cio San, to be in Part II of Act I: the aria *'Un bel dì'* (One fine day...). Here Cio-Cio San speaks the words of hope and confidence that her lover will return; but we in the audience already know that even as she sings, S.M. *Abraham Lincoln* is sailing into the bay with Captain Pinkerton and his American wife on board. Progressively through the aria the orchestra creates for us undercurrents of unease and rumblings of warning sounds which, in dialogue with Butterfly's song of love and hope, affect us most profoundly as we are already aware of her final tragic fate. In this context of meaning, Butterfly's aria becomes an ode to illusion that sustains a life in the house of bondage where she is waiting, trapped and suspended.

As we already know that considerable time has elapsed since Butterfly last saw her lover, the kind of perpetual pregnancy in Puccini's music here (cf. Grout, 1947) makes Butterfly's song a *cri de coeur* of all women whose lives have been defined by waiting since time immemorial: waiting for their men, husbands, sons, fathers, lovers and brothers to return from their labours, roamings and wars; waiting for their children to be born, for their bodies to go through their pre-determined phases; waiting for events outside their ken and control; waiting for one fine day... So, Butterfly also waits - she who is other than the man for whom she waits, not only different in her sex but also in the fundamental characteristic of race by virtue of which he is able to make a plaything of her, easily and without undue psychological discomfort. She is charming, guileless and literally childlike, as desirable women (as well as workers, black slaves and colonial natives - so de Beauvoir (1960) reminds us) have often been portrayed.

Yet Pinkerton feels, and in the end responds to, the power of the mystery which Butterfly, 'the love-sick little maiden' (Adami, 1973:155) represents for him; she remains unrevealed to him in her fecundity as in her death. Pinkerton's caddishness is typically masculine and his somewhat feeble suffering at the moment of Butterfly's tragic death, culturally incomprehensible though it must have been for him, is not simply a white man's guilt; rather, it is the suffering of all men who feel unable to reach into the impenetrable and inconceivable female psyche - so much the antithesis of her flesh - and are threatened by it. In this sense, Butterfly's kimono-clad image is a metaphor. She is the quintessential female figure - alien, oppressed, ignorant of the conditions which govern her existence, dependent -and yet, unfathomable and out of reach.

Puccini in effect turns a racial stereotype into an archetype. Butterfly's signature aria relies for its effect on our recognition of this at the level of responding with a complex of ideas, images and emotions which the music enables us to take a long way beyond the manifest content of the scene. When Butterfly sings the climactic refrain at the end of the aria: *'Io con sicura fede l'aspeto'* (I with unchangeable faith will await him), 'the music records a frenzied despair. Butterfly's subconscous mind is in a state of fear' (Osborne, 1982:168) and as the orchestra plays in the postlude, *fortissimo* and *largamente,* the melody of the first eight bars of the aria, the real meaning of Butterfly's song and of the image from which it emanates is finally delivered by the sound of the instruments to our already sensitised awareness.

For this interpretation to be feasible, it has to be assumed that Puccini has taken for granted, however unselfconsciously (as one does in the life-world), the connotations of race which his work evokes. His actual conscious intentions in this respect are, of course, inaccessible to us but we may imagine that the undercurrents of the meanings we perceive in the work to-day have been captured, even unwittingly, by the composer, as the creative process naturally interacts with submerged systems of socio-cultural relevancies. That is, the creative act connects previously unrelated dimensions of experience - initially at least at a sub-conscious level (cf. Koestler, 1966). Opera clearly bears out Koestler's contention that in this process 'the artist's aim... is to turn his audience into his accomplices (Koestler, 1966:403). That this can be achieved even posthumously is intelligible in the context of a cultural tradition which we assume can be seen as a continual selection and reselection of ancestors, interpreted through our own current experience (cf. Williams, 1980).

Of course none of this denies that music as sound is important in itself. But music as an experience, in relation to both the audience and the composer, is woven into the pattern of a total way of life which this inquiry presupposes to have some continuity between our time and that of the composer. His inspiration springs spontaneously from personal and social sources, however beholden for their expression these may be to means of technical and rational elaboration.

The artist's personal predilections will naturally influence the choice of significant themes and images to be elaborated in the work. Puccini was preoccupied with women - their nature, their eternal suffering and their voices. Part of this may have been due to his melancholy nature (cf. Adami, 1973); deep-seated psychological dynamics may have endowed him with heightened sensitivity to particular aspects of women's existence. It has even been suggested that there is a frequent conjunction of some of the greatest arias for his heroines with moments of their greatest debasement (as, for example, in *Tosca, Manon Lescaut* as well as in *Madam Butterfly*) (cf. Carner, 1958). Certainly in the scene where Butterfly sings *'Un bel di'*, her degradation is profound (more complete than when she dies at the end of the opera, rejected and hopeless, yet dignified). Here we perceive most sharply the self-deception and the powerlessness, born out by the futility of her arduous vigil which at times the orchestra conspiratoriously communicates to an audience that already shares with the composer the secret of Butterfly's fate. We already understand, much better than Butterfly, that she is the victim of the contradictions of love, extrinsic in terms of the strains on social bonds that love almost always entails, and intrinsic in its inherent ambivalence.

In so far as imputed inferiority is an aspect of racial stereotyping, Butterfly's Japanese-ness adds another dimension to the associative links in the audience's consciousness through which her complex plight is felt. There is a dialectic between these dimensions of the scene and some of the musical moments of the aria which consist of great climactic surges, with orchestra and voice both alternating and acting in unison. This dialectic brings to mind Freud's view regarding the great orgasmic potential of a debased sexual object: '...the man almost always feels his respect for the woman acting as a restriction on his sexual activity; and only develops full (physical and psychic) potency when he is with a debased sexual object' (Freud, 1977:254). If this is a significant aspect of sexuality, it suggests a psychological dimension the recognition (perhaps unconscious) of which may have enabled Puccini to portray so incisively the objectification of Butterfly.

The theoretical terms of the foregoing discussion are very general and its example is limited in scope. Such a configuration suits the two main intentions of this paper: first, the broad theoretical references merely raise the possibility of a sociological approach to the meaning of opera which attends to music as a significant aspect of the process within which this meaning is produced; and secondly, the single example in its complexity may suggest that no general pattern can be expected to account for the way in which aspects of race and gender are absorbed, fused and reflected in cultural forms.

Bibliography

Adami, G.R. (ed) (1973) *Letters of Giacomo Puccini;* English translation and edition by Ena Makin, New York, Vienna House.
Adorno, T. (1976) *Introduction to the Sociology of Music,* New York, Seabury Press.
Carner, M. (1958) *Puccini; A Critical Biography,* London, Duckworth.
de Beauvoir, S. (1960) *The Second Sex,* London, Faber & Faber.
Donnington, R. (1981) *The Rise of Opera,* London, Faber & Faber.
Drummond, J.D. (1980) *Opera in Perspective,* London, J.M. Dart.
Freud, S. (1977) 'On the Universal Tendency to Debasement in the Sphere of Love' in A. Richards (ed) *The Pelican Freud Library,* Vol. 7, Harmondsworth, Penguin.
Grout, D.J. (1965) *A Short History of Opera,* Oxford University Press, 2nd ed.
Kerman, J. (1956) *Opera as Drama,* New York, Vintage Books.
Koestler, A. (1966) *The Act of Creation,* London, Pan Books, 2nd ed.
Osborne, C. (1982) *The Complete Operas of Puccini,* New York, Athenaeum.
Schutz, A. (1964) 'On Multiple Realities' in A. Schutz *Collected Papers,* Vol. II, The Hague, Nijhoff.
Schutz, A. (1976) 'Fragments on the Phenomenology of Music', *Music and Man,* Vol. 2, Nos. 1/ 2.
Schutz, A. (1978) 'Phenomenology and the Social Sciences' in T. Luckman (ed) *Phenomenology and Sociology,* Harmondsworth, Penguin.
Skadra, C. (1979) 'Alfred Schutz's Phenomenology of Music', *Journal of Musicological Research,* Vol. 3.
Supicic, I. (1970) 'Matter and form in Music', *International Review of Music, Aesthetics and Sociology,* Vol. 1, No. 2.
Williams, R. (1980) *The Long Revolution,* Harmondsworth, Penguin.

Race Renounced, Culture Arraigned: The Case of the So-Called Culture-Bound Psychoses

Barbara Lovric

Scanning the literature on culture and disease in developing regions of the world, one is struck by a peculiar paralogism. Ethnopsychiatric studies and psychodynamic anthropological formulations suggest that the ills of the impoverished are largely psychogenic, psychosomatic and culture-induced. A high frequency of mental disease, once linked to racial infantile mentality, is now imputed to a 'cultural personality' generally predisposed to a poor tolerance of anxiety, to somatising social distress and conflict, or to acting out unresolved tension through aggressive panic or hysterical deviance (cf. Stoller 1969; Wittkower and Termanson 1969; Obeysekere 1970, 1977; Leighton 1982; Kleinman 1980). The high incidence of diseases manifesting mental symptoms among populations of Southeast Asia in general and the poor in particular is indisputable. But is a significant proportion of this morbidity actually due to a kind of cultural deficit? What of the ecological, biochemical and genetic factors involved in the dynamics of mental disorder?

Unfamiliar magico-medical rituals, assumptions concerning the supernatural and a set of bizarre symptoms and signs among the local populations of colonised Southeast Asia attracted the attention and imagination of Westerners who observed them or read about them. Local names (e.g. *amok* and *latah*) were retained in many accounts and experts in the field, such as Yap (1967:173), considered it essential to integrate these 'exotic syndromes' into recognised (Western) classification and standard nomenclature. When clinical manifestations were not directly equatable with anything described in Western medical experience, the syndromes were labelled 'atypical culture-bound variants of reactive syndromes' (Yap 1967:175). Deviations from Western definitions of abnormality were aberrations.

Paradoxically, culturally defined witches and demons and related fears and anxieties, together with possession affliction syndromes and voluntary trance states, are all accommodated within this classification of culture-bound psychogenic psychoses (cf. Leff 1981:16). But in indigenous magico-medical experience and classification these phenomena may be attributed to three clearly differentiated categories. In the Balinese context, witch fear and anxiety (which pertain to illnesses of which they are imputed agents) is normal and rational. Involuntary affliction possession (such as *babainan*) is disease. Voluntary trance states are not. In terms of aesthetics and function, volitional, controlled possession states are unlike non-volitional possession affliction such as *babainan* which is a manifestation of pathology. The fact that voluntary possession states served the interests of the community was no argument against their abnormality, or so Yap ruled (1967:175).

This ascription of abnormality to actions proceeding from indigenous epistemological assumptions about supernaturally-endowed agents in the spread of disease and human mystical participation with the supernatural, together with the denial of a possible organic basis to unfamiliar forms of morbidity among different (Asian and non-Judeo-Christian) populations, promoted Western attempts to diagnose whole cultures psychiatrically, if not psychotically. Postulating a category of culture-bound syndromes meant that indigenous medical ideologies, repressive social structures and culture predilections generated their own forms of morbidity. But such studies have not led to a satisfactory understanding of all the problems and patterns of morbidity in Asian populations. Instead, what they highlight is a problem, particularly in psychoanalytically-oriented paradigms constructed to explain these conditions.

Although not addressing the more complex issue of transcultural psychiatric research, Ellard offered the following warning which is relevant to the present issue:

> One of the deadly charms of psychiatry is that being a subject without boundaries it encourages the contemplation of large and complicated questions. This in turn provides an opportunity of reaching magnificent, all embracing answers, so reducing human complexity to such pellucid insights as to cause all to marvel. The unfortunate result is that not only does speculation proliferate while the answers remain elusive, but also after a time the speculations become mistaken for the answers, and we arrive at exquisitely fashioned shadows with no substance in them (1985:17).

It is possible that some forms of culture-bound syndromes are atypical variations of Western forms of psychogenic psychoses. It is equally possible that they are morbid conditions without any clear Western medical counterparts. To confine the labelling of them to Western psychiatric nosology is perhaps to miss their actual as well as their putative significance.

106

The uneasy interface in Western medical discourse between neurology and psychiatry (specialties addressing organically based and functionally based mental disturbance respectively) is not apparent in the study of syndromes such as *babainan* among Asian populations. Only one aspect is represented and it is in no way neurologically or even biologically inclined. These studies rely on the conceptual frameworks, axioms and implications familiar to Western social psychiatry and psychoanalytical anthropology (cf. Surya 1969). Psychiatry's incursions into sociology, and the reverse, are reflected in these formulations. Mental disease has been a particularly fertile source of debate and disagreement and, allied to the notions of race and culture, it becomes an even greater polemic, one to which I shall return in the final section of this paper.

I turn now to discuss Balinese *babainan*, a culture-bound functional disorder, according to the Western formulations mentioned above, but labelled aetiologically as possession affliction and defined as organic illness in indigenous medical theory. When I refer to Javanese *latah*, later in this paper, I refer back to the lesser known (outside Bali) *babainan* in order to question the validity of the use Westerners have made of, first, race and then culture as significant contributory factors in the genesis of disorders which essentially belong to the category of phenomena-not-yet-understood.

(i) Babainan; Case Studies

In Balinese cognisance and medical discourse, to be afflicted by a virulent, live magical spell called *babai* through the intermediary of a witch *(leyak)* is to suffer an organic illness named *babainan*. Depending on the peculiar nature of the 'invading organism' *(babai)* and the tissues or organ wherein it settles, symptoms and signs ranging from mild physical discomfort to severe mental distress ensue. The disease may present as an acute episode, quickly resolved or, more frequently, as a chronic illness with acute episodes. In terms of diagnoses by *balian* (healers) - and less than 2 percent of the population have their illnesses diagnosed by Western-style doctors *(Bali Post* 22 October 1976) - it is among the most frequently occurring diseases. It is also one of the most feared and dreaded. The disorder is not of recent origin. Local medical texts *(usada)* describe the aetiology, pathogenesis, clinical manifestations and treatment for *babainan*. Case examples from fieldwork where I observed *balian* at work convey some notion of the form and context of *babai* affliction:

1. 20/ 11/ 81 The illness from which a man in his middle fifties was suffering was diagnosed as *babainan*. His main symptoms were weakness, palpitations, aching pains in the limbs and difficult micturition. He had already been to a local health clinic but, allegedly, the cause of his discomfort had not been determined nor had a diagnosis been made. He had con-

sulted the healer several times previously, and the severity of his symptoms tended to fluctuate. This time the *balian* prescribed medical therapy in the form of mantra, ablution with purified water, the ingestion of an incinerated magical drawing and the inhalation of burning incense among other things. Thereafter the *balian* took a black peppercorn and pressed it into each of the man's finger tips in turn. He was searching for evidence of the area of activity of the *babai*. Wherever the procedure induced no pain, the *babai* was deemed to be no longer active in that portion of the body. The *balian* then took a piece of black wood, held it over burning incense, breathed upon it and placed it between the man's third and fourth toes, pressing the toes inward against the piece of wood. The man writhed in apparent pain and cried out. This was, it seemed, the point of entry and the focus of activity of the virulent *babai*. The *balian* continued applying what did not seem to me to be very strong pressure to the toes for a few seconds longer and the man continued to moan and cry out begging him to cease.

Finding the exact location of the *babai* and compelling it to acknowledge its presence, which it had done through the cries of the man, was not tantamount to a resolution of the sickness. It was only the beginning. The man would return to the *balian* several times more to build up his own strength and resistance. Ideally, in time, the *babai* would concede defeat and announce its intention of relinquishing its hold on the body. I was told that this was a very severe case of *babainan:* the *babai* had been created on Lombok and at times the man suffered nervous symptoms such as moodiness and disorientation when the *babai* moved from the lower part of his body up to his head.

2. 24/ 1/ 82 A woman in her early thirties with three children had been ill on and off for seven years and had been to the hospital 'for injections'. Her illness was diagnosed by the *balian* as *babainan*. She complained of weakness in her legs and severe pain behind her eyes and sometimes in her head. Her husband explained that she was often listless and without energy. The treatment procedure was essentially the same as that already described. The *balian* also applied a concoction, consisting of oil from a species of freshwater fish and spices, to the woman's eyes. Pain behind the eyes was the symptom which apparently bothered her most. She cried out during this treatment and then kept spitting for some time after. I was told that if there had not been a *babai* there she would not have experienced such violent reaction. The pepper and wood application to the hands and feet had not elicited any pain reaction. The *babai* had already moved from those locations.

3. 21/ 10/ 81 An eighteen year old male was diagnosed as suffering from *babainan desti*. This name referred to the mechanism *(desti)* whereby he

contracted the illness. The affliction was also named *babai bongol* because at one stage deafness *(bongol)* represented the dominant symptom. At another phase of the illness, that of active delirium, he had run away aimlessly. The illness had then been renamed to indicate a particular manifestation of mental disturbance. At this stage the boy was in an abnormally agitated and frightened state and looked dazed and disoriented. I learned later that, in what had seemed to me to be no more than confused muttering, the *babai* had acknowledged and named a local *balian* as its 'owner'. The *babai* requested that a ritual be conducted at the graveyard on its behalf. The request was agreed to and fulfilled. The *babai* 'disappeared' and in time the boy became symptom-free.

4. 5/ 2/ 82 A twenty-three year old woman related the events surrounding her illness with a kind of detachment one might expect of a disinterested spectator. She had been feeling quite well and then one night shortly after going to bed she suddenly started raving and hallucinating. She was admitted to hospital under a *doktor syaraf* (nerve doctor) and 'given injections'. The visual and auditory hallucinations and the raving ceased. She was discharged from hospital but the symptoms recurred. She was then taken to a *balian* and given the standard treatment. Apart from the disturbance of consciousness, she also remembered that when she was in the acute stage of the illness her body seemed to be grossly enlarged and at times she was unable to walk.

The ravings of the *babainan* sufferer are not considered to be their own but those of the living *babai* spirit. The objective of sometimes violent questioning and treatment is to induce the *babai* to name its purchaser or, less frequently, its owner-creator. No formal redress is sought by the *balian* and no moral judgement is pronounced. The sociological significance of *babainan,* I suggest, lies in its imputed aetiology and treatment, namely, in the complex of suspicions and manipulations inherent in illness episodes and the powers of the creators of *babai* on the other. I forego such an analysis here in favour of a more cognitive study and a search for a meaning of the phenomenon itself which is consistent with the medical data that local texts yield.

(ii) The Creation and Path of the Pathogen (Babai Spell)
The term *babai* is cognate with *bayi* meaning 'foetus'. It denotes a magical spell, the most potent form of which is concocted around an aborted foetus, a stillborn infant or a placenta. A *babai* is not ambiguous; its virulence is unequivocal. Its reason-for-being is to induce disease in its human host. In some respects *babai* is not unlike the Malay concept of*badi* (cf. Endicott 1970:69-83) which, according to Endicott, represents the loss of control, the crucial boundary between life and death. Its exceedingly malignant, marginal and uncontrollable nature renders it an object of fear.

The only ambivalence associated with *badi* (and the same applies to *babai*) is that it does not clearly belong within either the category of supernaturals or humans.

However, *babai* also share characteristics with the Malay *pelesit* which is a familiar spirit acquired through the magical manipulations over a corpse of an infant who was the first-born of first-born parents. A common form of spirit affliction during pregnancy, the *pelesit* is imputed to enter the body through the feet causing the victim to scream with pain and lose consciousness. Like the *babai,* it is exorcised through mantra and demands that it should reveal, through the mouth of its host, the identity of its 'parents' (owners). If this fails to elicit a confession, the Malay *bomor* (shaman) applies pressure to the fingers and the toes of the afflicted and carries out an interrogation until the *pelesit* finally confesses and agrees to leave (Gimlette 1923:42-3; Endicott 1970:57).

Marginality and ambiguity are characteristics of things magically powerful and dangerous in Balinese thought. Foetal material, post-partum and menstrual blood, matters which pertain to life and procreation, are all imputed to represent the most potent sources of power for the creation of *babai.* The products of miscarriages procured for the purposes of creating *babai* are placed in containers and buried in graveyards, spiritually nurtured and given offerings as well as life-cycle rites. They are also finally taken to temples associated with the powers of death where, through the intercession of the Goddess of Death, Bhatari Durga, they receive their power and privilege and become her representatives. The abundance of information concerning the actual procuring and raising of a *babai* testifies to the extent to which the phenomenology of the symptom complex, which the Balinese term *babainan,* has influenced an elaboration of its aetiology (cf. Weck 1937:205-12).

Though treatment aims ultimately to rid the body of the *babai,* immediate expulsion is not considered a possibility. Medicinal therapy, offerings and mantra to deities of fire, such as Agni and Brahma, anticipate a gradual weakening of the *babai's* hold within the body of the host. An extinction or even permanent extrusion of the *babai* is not presumed a likely resolution to *babainan* affliction. Mantra prescribed to prevent, contain and reverse *babai* affliction are numerous. Requisite ingredients are copious and expensive, consisting of animal, vegetable and mineral origins, either buried, formed into a potion or applied to the afflicted.

Allusions in the treatments to a flaming, burning and fiery resolution of *babai* intrusion are prominent. In the form of therapy called *tutuhan* the *babai* is expected to react to the heat and burning caused by the concoction applied to the eyes of the afflicted. Mantra are frequently addressed to

Brahma whose colour is red and whose quality is fire (cf. HKS2183:20a). Magical drawings used in association with mantra to expel or incinerate *babai* display a fairly distinctive but limited range of motifs. Mystical syllables and geometric forms based upon the emblems of the deities of the nine directions feature prominently. Mystical syllables are usually found in association with a flaming human head. Composite human-animal representations of demonic appearance are used in conjunction with mantra invoking the powers of high deities so that the virulence of the *babai* is extinguished (K422:10,5). To prevent the access of *babai* into a houseyard, a piece of copper one hand-span in length and three fingers in width, on to which a magical drawing of the Yama-Raja figure is inscribed, should be buried in the middle of the yard. The Yama-Raja figure, a grossly enlarged part-animal part-human form, perhaps representative of the visual hallucinations and distorted perceptions of *babainan* affliction (see case study 4), is a conspicuous part of the imagery of physical and mental pathology. Perhaps the most distinctive magical drawing associated specifically with *babainan* is that named *bawange*. It should be inscribed upon an onion and buried below the sleeping platform of one possessed of *babai* (cf. HKS3124:4b). Some similarity to a developing embryo (the position and unequal development of limbs notwithstanding) or a malformed one might be intended.

The presumed existence of people capable of acquiring the knowledge and means of creating *babai,* and thereby insidious and debilitating forms of disease among individuals, is an obvious source of anxiety among the population. There are descriptions of *babai* created on the nearby island of Lombok through the sexual union of male and female witches. Such *babai* might have the form of an infant with a grossly enlarged head, exhibit facial and cranial features of a cat or a monkey and produce a cry reminiscent of sounds normally produced by ducks. Animal imagery is a constant element in Balinese medical phenomena.

What also invites thought and begs elucidation is the prominence of human stillbirth, miscarriage and missed-conceptions (menstrual blood) in indigenous aetiologic conceptions. The mystical power of the human embryo, the potential of menstrual blood and the anomalous nature and magical potency of a fresh human corpse in general, and of a stillborn in particular, are discernible themes of Balinese magico-medical theory and practices.

Interestingly, supernaturals who participate with humanity in voluntary trance possession are commonly 'child-like' in manner and name. Infants or 'small humans' also feature prominently in graphic representations of mystical agents involved in the pathogenic process. The key to the symbolism in the *bawange* drawing may lie in a specific form of foetal malformation perceived to be caused by amnion rupture during gestation. Foetal digits or members (such as a foot or an arm) *in utero* can become entwined by fibrous strands resulting in constriction bands and leading to partial or complete amputations. The subject of amniogenic foetal malformations is one of the oldest medical mysteries (Torpin 1968:4).

Possibly, the peculiar status of the unborn foetus, neither ordinary human nor supernatural, is the basis of this particular archetype and analogical signification. The semiotics of *babai* as a supernatural pathological agent might perhaps then be understood through the notion of projection and dialectical reversal. That is, *babai* project a reality - high infant mortality rate, miscarriage, foetal malformations, stillbirths and infertility - superimposed upon or transcoded within another, namely, a ubiquitous and analagous form of morbidity which commonly manifests only after puberty. Elsewhere (Lovric 1987b) I argue that the symbolism in other prominent cultural representations also encode morbid realities.

Local understanding and theory of *babainan* is based upon intimate experience and keen observation. Forasmuch as the disease is attributed at one level of causation to *babai* (an 'irrational' proposition in Western scientific thought), this is no reason to discount local classifications and symptomatology as being devoid of clinical significance, or to relegate the syndrome wholly to the psychosocial arena.

(iii) The Medical Semiology of an 'Exotic' Syndrome
A manuscript transliteration (HKS2183) of a Balinese medical text entitled *Tingkah ing Ngubah Babai,* 'Procedure for the Raising of Babai' tells us that:

> ...there are *babai* without form, without abodes, emerging through desire, through thought, through the mind, the breath and speech...

Knowledge of the unmanifest potent endowment of *babai* which produce disease includes the following;

> I Mjajapati becomes *pamali* [a disease spell] causing a stabbing pain, returns to its place of origin and becomes the *babai* named I Truna Bagus causing pain and manifesting as an illness named *lara buh*['swelling affliction'].

> I Anggapati becomes *dengen* [a disease spell] and settles under the chest causing migratory severe stabbing pain. It eventually settles in the abdomen and then returns to its abode in the soil and an illness named *tiwang* [convulsive seizures] appears.

> I Amad is able to create a disease in which symptoms persist for many years.

> If the afflicted person cries and screams, I Mlata has created the disease.

If the afflicted person remains silent, withdrawn, quiet and mute and is oedemic, I Bongol has made the disease.

If the afflicted person compulsively utters incantations and prays using meaningless phrases, Sang Ermas, the *ratu* of all *babai* is responsible for the disease.

I Jinjin creates a disease which manifests with confusion.

I Buk creates a disease which manifests with tingling sensations and pain in all the joints.

I Bodo causes generalised pain.

I Ariman is able to cause death.

When a wide range of symptoms and signs are displayed by the afflicted, the illness is named I Mas-Rejek-Gumi who has thirty dynamic manifestations. Each pursues a different pathway, settles in a different location in the body and causes changing symptoms. Tests state that there are thirty-three forms of *babai* and a similar number of locations in the body where they are apt to settle. The signal cue about the differences in kind pertains to the form in which the disease presents and the location of distress in the body.

Baltan also refer to other *babai* named according to the symptoms they cause. *Babai Dewa* causes its host to speak in a high-pitched voice and to pray all the time, that is act as though possessed by a deity (when one is not). *Babai Amuk* causes its host to speak crudely, act defiantly, seize weapons and attack others randomly and without cause. *Babai Ganjah* causes a loss of memory and aimless roaming. *Babai Asmara* causes uncontrollable and unprovoked laughter. *Babai Negul* causes pain in the chest. The most potent *babai*, alleged to originate on Lombok, enters the body and causes gross swelling of the abdomen.

Another text on *babainan*, sundry neurological and somatic symptoms and herbal treatments, entitled Usada Sasah, lists a further group of *babainan* manifestations; confusion, hazy vision, ringing sensations in the ears, coldness (beginning in the feet and gradually enveloping the whole body), fear, terrifying visual hallucinations, epigastric and abdominal pain, uncontrollable crying and yelling followed by withdrawal and unnatural quietness.

The texts state that the illness has no one single cause as manifestations and presentation of it are varied and manifold. It may begin in the lower abdomen with sharp pain as if something is being thrust into that part of the body. The pain appears suddenly and recurs intermittently. It may move to the centre of the abdomen, then on to the liver. When the *babai* moves to the head, the afflicted becomes dizzy, hallucinates and behaves like one insane. Such a person may become unconscious. When the neck is the location of the *babai*, it becomes swollen, stiff and sore, its vessels become rigid and swollen and the afflicted is unable to speak. Feelings of suffocation and choking may follow. If the tongue becomes the location of the *babai,* the afflicted behaves like one possessed by deities, speaking in a high-pitched sweet tone. They are weak and lethargic and stagger when walking (K422; HKS113,7; HKS2184).

The maintenance of normal body temperature (lack of fever) is a defining feature of *babainan*, according to *balian*. The major manifestations classified as belonging to the *babainan* symptom complex do not generally occur during the febrile phase of an illness. This seems to differentiate *babainan from tiwang* (infective neuropathies) and to place it closer to syndromes included in the *tujuj* (nutritional neuropathies) category. There is patently some overlap which has been observed and documented (cf., HKS3097). In both categories of disease there are manifestations of central nervous system disturbance and sensory and motor manifestations of peripheral neuropathy (progressive paralysis, paraesthesis, for example).

Have the Balinese fabricated this symptom syndrome and diligently recorded it in their medical manuscripts? Or have they observed a seemingly related spectrum of disorders with mental, sensory and motor symptoms and recorded them under the generic aetiologic name *babainan*? In Balinese medical theory, the syndrome is not mere psychogenic reaction.

To transpose this indigenous recording of a syndrome into Western medical parlance, *babainan* manifests with physical, sensory or mental symptoms, or all three. The most characteristic somatic features of the disease are swelling, often of the abdomen, partial facial swelling and palsy, migratory sub-cutaneous nodules often located around the neck or limbs and itchy skin lesions. Pain, weakness and partial temporary and recurrent paralysis are the major symptoms and signs. Sensations of numbness, tingling, burning and prickling are common. Pain, of a sharp, shooting or stinging quality is located most frequently in the epigastrium, lower abdomen, neck, throat, eyes, head and joints. Mental symptoms cover a wide range of perceptual and cognitive impairment and distortion of consciousness ranging from partial loss of awareness to complete confusion, stupor and temporary loss of consciousness. Tremors and partial and generalised spasms described under the generic diagnostic category of *tiwang* are generally absent from the *babainan* symptom complex. Violent motor excitement, nodding of the head, rhythmic moving of the eyes, grasping and sucking reflexes, characteristic of *tuju* and *tiwang* symptomatology, are also absent from local descriptions of *babainan*.

The multi-dimensional *babai* is the imputed initiator of a wide spectrum of pathologic conditions. *Babainan*, the symptom complex itself, enjoys remarkable notoriety but it is not a highly communicable disease. There is no mention in the texts of epidemics with associated high mortality rates, but it is endemic and a common cause of morbidity. *Balian* concede that it is one of the most difficult to treat of the theoretically curable diseases; some people afflicted with the condition recover in a few days while others remain afflicted for months, years or a life-time. *Balian* do not consider *babainan* to have a higher incidence among women, nor is it a disease of neonates and infants. It occurs only rarely among children. *Balian* handle most cases of *babainan*. Western-type doctors do not generally claim to understand the disease; the syndrome is not described as such in the Western medical textbooks. 'Scientific' interest in indigenous medical knowledge does not extend much beyond a search for possible benefits of 'unknown' (miracle) herbal remedies.

On the basis of comparative data and the trend in Western studies referred to earlier, psychodynamic theorists posit that Balinese medical ideology, concern with witches and demons and social repression have created a culture-bound reactive psychosis. In the limited range of material on the subject, *babainan* is situated in the ethnopsychiatric model of 'madness' which rejects a bio-medical paradigm for the study of psychiatric morbidity, supporting instead the Laingian psychological credo that mental disorder should not be regarded as disease but an intelligible reaction to insane sociocultural arrangements. That is, those diagnosed as suffering from psychological dysfunction are actually the 'blessed mad' with special insight: *babainan* symptoms in this model represent 'one response to a wide range of transient and ongoing stress in Balinese social life' and the condition is a means of releasing violent emotions strongly suppressed in the context of culture (Connor 1982:785).

A local non-Balinese Western-style doctor told me that she treated *babainan* 'Christian-style', with injections and Christian prayers. She suggested that the 'Balinese religion contributed to *babainan* because of belief in evil spirits'. In her estimation, *balian* cannot distinguish between neurosis, psychosis and epilepsy, but lump them all together as *babainan*. A non-Balinese Western-style psychiatrist practising on Bali (personal communication) does not consider *babainan* to be the exotic syndrome it is alleged to be but says the term covers a wider field than psychiatric disorder. Many such acute illnesses can be classified as *babainan* and he proposed that there may be two forms of *babainan*, an organically based and a functional one. This may represent a satisfactory compromise explanation for the syndrome.

Excluding for a moment the manifestations of mental derangement, the sensory and motor symptoms of *babainan* can be considered alongside such Western clinical categories as peripheral neuropathies and parasitic disease, the aetiology of which is associated with infection and nutritional rather than socio-cultural deficiencies. In the tropics, the causes (besides beriberi and pellagra which I have identified as of the *tuju* category of disease) of peripheral neuropathy are legion although uncertain (Maegraith 1984:334). The invasion of the human body by helminths (parasitic worms) may cause symptoms ranging from skin lesions to dementia. Obscure spastic paraplegias are common in South India (Taori and Iyer 1973). Paraplegias of unknown origin, reported from parts of Africa, are believed to be nutritional in origin (Weatheral 1983:21,149-57).

The syndrome of tropical ataxic neuropathy, described in certain Asian and African communities, commonly present with various forms of paraesthesiae in the extremities. Blurring of vision, ringing sounds in the ears (tinnitus), deafness, weakness, unsteadiness of gait and colicky abdominal pain are common symptoms. The syndrome may result from dietary deficiencies, viral infections or primary genetic factors. The condition generally affects males and females equally around the fifth decade of life (Weatherall et al., 1983:21, 154). A juvenile form of motor neurone disease, where the average age of onset is 15 years, has been described in South India. The condition is characterised by weakness of the limbs, difficulty in swallowing, atrophy of the tongue and bilateral (nerve) deafness. Observable and palpable twitching of muscles in the extremities is common (Wadia 1973:21, 152). Sensory impairment of polyneuropathies usually involves the hands and lower limbs. Touching the skin can aggravate paraesthesiae. Stimuli normally not painful can cause unpleasant sensations and repeated stimulation in the same place may cause pain to spread and reach intolerable intensities. The clinical presentation therefore of some cases of *babainan* and symptomatology of *babainan* as presented in local medical writings suggest possible parallels with these kinds of physiological stress.

As mentioned, part of the *babainan* diagnostic strategy employed by *balian* involves pressing stimuli in the form of a peppercorn or a sharp piece of wood against the fingers, toes or soles of the feet. Pain arising from such stimulation indicates the presence of the pathogen *(babai)*. An appropriate mantra is uttered and thus it becomes a diagnostic tool through which the *balian* traces the position of the *babai* within the body. Presuming that these practices do indicate some neuropathological disease, albeit not explained in Western terms, I suggest that a classic peculiarity of a frequent symptom has been encoded in a traditional magico-medical technique.

One might also wonder if the migratory swellings or nodules, also part of the confirmatory symptomatology of *babainan,* indicate reactions to parasitic nematode (worm) infections. Moderately severe cases of larval hookworm disease produce visceral symptoms, marked weakness, rapid fatigue, dizziness, tinnitus, headache and palpitations. Severe infection causes intensification of the symptoms together with oedema, abdominal distention, epigastric pain, abnormal perverted taste, breathlessness, paraesthesiae, depression and syncope. Paraesthesias, consisting of exaggerated sensitivity to touch, are a clinical expression of other nematode infections.

Human infestation with the encysted larvae of the pork tapeworm *(taenia solium)* is characterised by variable and unpredictable symptoms of motor and sensory disorder and painless subcutaneous nodules due to the localisation of calcified cysts. Psychiatric symptoms may develop as an isolated syndrome, varying widely from simple hallucinations, slow-mindedness, emotional disturbance to confusion, apathy, global amnesia and dementia. These may be transient or develop progressively. The fatality rate in untreated symptomatic cases exceeds five percent. The survival time varies from a few minutes to thirty-five years from the onset of the first symptom (Warren and Mahmoud, 1984). Filarasis, a highly prevalent form of worm infection produces in different hosts a broad range of clinical manifestations. Thus, it is suggested that a variety of disorders may be diagnosed as *babainan.* Here I have shifted into a Western medical frame of reference because I perceive no alternative means through which to investigate the problem of a not-yet-understood phenomenon and the epistemological basis of *babainan* symbolism, although I recognise another way of knowing, another epistemology and another way of encoding reality. What I have done is place the symbolism of *babainan* in a context and I have sought relational meanings.

The proposition of physiological aetiology should not be seen as contradicting the *balian* construction of *babainan,* for this itself has constituted my primary analytical data. Moreover, it is essential to think about other ways of knowing and about the cultural expressions and elaborations woven around the disease experience, and to seek to understand the logic in other classificatory systems, descriptions of symptomatology, diagnostic processes and forms of treatment. When similar motifs and symbols in various local constructions of disease are found among peoples at a similar level of technological development, who are also vulnerable to similar microbes and the effects of malnutrition and infection, some consideration may also be given to the capacity of the pathological process itself to inspire symbolism.

A related matter I wish to stress is the lack of Western understanding of tropical neurology. Exceedingly complex problems await neurological research in tropical Asia (cf. Wadia 1973; Spillane 1974; Edington and Gilles 1976; Brown and Voge 1982) where there is a high incidence of some recognised neurological conditions and of as-yet-undescribed conditions:

> The assemblage [there] of clinical material is more glaring than in a temperate environment and the diagnosis is often harder to achieve. The visitor's outstanding impressions are likely to be two-fold: the gross affliction of the stricken and the obscurity of many of their illnesses (Spillane 1974:269)

Descriptive neurology, like psychiatry, is largely based upon experience in temperate climates in technologically advanced cultures among nutritionally advantaged populations where sanitation is adequate and parasitic infections are not common. Even the limited range of colonial medical investigations and interventions on small and unrepresentative samples of colonised populations yielded awareness of obscure forms of morbidity. I suggest therefore, that syndromes such as *babainan* may express gross manifestations of central nervous system and peripheral nervous system dysfunction which are no longer familiar to Western nosography, or perhaps have never been part of the symptomatology of nervous disorders in temperate Western regions. Those approaches based on the hypothesis that syndromes such as *babainan* are psychosocial in origin, and therefore a product of cultural dysfunction, are perhaps a consequence of the tendency of the social sciences to avoid physiology (see Fabrega 1977:274; Freeman 1983:294).

In the section below, I use the well-studied case of another culture-bound syndrome, that of *latah,* through which to demonstrate my assertions. There is an extensive literature on *latah* (cf. Winzeler, 1984) but no indigenous data.

(iv) The Problem of Not-Yet-Understood Ethno-medical Phenomena; The Comparative Case of Javanese Latah

Unfamiliar forms of morbidity encountered by Europeans in colonised regions sometimes presented an affront to their codes of ethics and etiquette. Interest in and concern for their medical implications came much later if at all. There is no mention in the colonial medical literature of *babainan*. Although the colonial medical discourse on culture-bound syndromes such as *latah* and *amok* was carried out largely by medically-trained observers who acknowledged the importance of infections, especially malaria, as exciting causes, they nevertheless retained the notionthat some residual (evolutionary) endogenic psychical processes contributed to these diseases.

Latah is a specific syndrome characterised by an abnormal startle reaction,

118

fearfulness, loss of control, hypersuggestability and temporary dissociation. Pallor, palpitations, shaking, groping and scratching movements with the hands may also be present. A disturbance of language ability takes various forms such as meaningless utterances or lavatory babble (coprolalia), fornication babble (pornolalia), involuntary blurting of crude sexual terms, phrases or suggestions, verbal mimicry (echolalia) and bodily mimicry (echopraxia). In addition, automatic obedience can also be a confirmatory sign of the affliction. The immediate exciting causes may be auditory, visual or tactile, and symptoms may be preceded by an initial dream, sometimes of an erotic nature.

Colonial observers did not seriously consider ecological and bio-medical factors or the possibility of organic dysfunction of the nervous system in *latah* crises. Instead, they postulated the existence of innate racial psychical qualities, or that the crises related to 'untrained mentality', 'infantile-primitiveness' and such-like (van Loon 1924; Theunissen 1921; Fitzgerald 1923). As Yap notes, Scheube (1903) included *latah* along the sprue and dysentery under a chapter title of organic diseases of tropical regions and Mansell labelled it a 'pathogenic disease' peculiar to 'barbarous and semi-civilised countries' and to the 'weak-minded of the advanced ones' (Yap 1952:517-24). According to Winzeler, Clifford (1898) criticised medical interpretations of *latah* for lacking what he perceived as humanistic concern, and provided instead the explanation that the Malay character was rooted in morbid nervousness (Winzeler 1983:83-5). Travaglino (1920:38) concluded that the Javanese and kindred races were 'psychotically and morbidly emotional' and Fitzgerald noted that '*latah* is due to suggestion in an impressionable, neurotic, and weak-minded person...' (1923:155). In other words, people exhibiting probable signs of disturbance of the nervous system (including epileptiform illness and encephalitis) were all classified as lunatics. The colonisers built asylums and confidently postulated that all their health problems would soon be overcome if only the natives would learn to wear shoes and be 'more like us'.

Yap, a British-trained psychiatrist, who wrote extensively on culture-bound syndromes, saw *latah* as a form of fright neurosis, culturally determined and maintained among those hypersensitive to fright and whose defenses were limited by the level of their cultural and technological development (1952:560). He suggested that the adoption of bizarre behavioural symptoms was the only recourse available to 'psychologically disorganised individuals' and to those with 'weak egos':

> The untutored person in Malay society, especially in the case of females, is a shy, retiring, unaggressive, self-effacing changeable and colourless person, with little individuality (Yap 1952:553).

119

Using a more explicit evolutionary (racist and sexist) paradigm, another colonial observer explained fright reactions and assumed higher frequencies among women thus:

> ...The higher a people is civilised, the more controlled are its affect-reactions; we also see the more intellectually developed individual stand farther away from the 'wild' type than the undeveloped. These latter have a more 'infantile' way of reacting; therefore the civilised man stands farthest away; the woman whose entire psyche remains at a more infantile stage than that of the man (strongly emotional, suggestible etc.), in the same way shows a stronger affect reaction. Thus it is not surprising that especially the primitive woman of the lower classes shows pathological anomalies in this direction... (van Loon 1924:315).

In an article entitled 'Contributions to the Knowledge of Indian Psychoses', Theunissen posited 'important differences' between 'less developed people' and 'more cultured man' and concluded that 'from an intellectual point of view' the average native mind was inferior to the European, being 'slow and poor in ideas' (1921:79, 85). Furthermore, he maintained that the natives' apprehensions about evil spirits were relevant to their character and their mental diseases. Nevertheless, he held that intoxication and infection were the direct cause of psychoses (Theunissen, 1921:81).

Apparently, the odd neurologist who happened upon the scene classified *latah* as a neurological disease (due to degeneration of the brain) and thereby, in Yap's judgement, departed from intelligent psychological speculation which emphasised the common initial 'sexual' or 'phallic' dream about dismembered, erect and gross penises (1952:524). Freudian interpretations argued that the dream, its imagery and imputed cause (sexual frustration and repression) were precipitating factors in the emergence of *latah*. But this seems to me to confuse the effect with the cause as vivid, frightening dreams can constitute prodromal symptoms of organic psychosis. Like Kenny (1978), I would also relate the significance of the initial disturbing dream content to local constructions of disease spirits and magical symbolism. Interestingly, in an earlier colonial observation, sexual repression was not seen to be an issue:

> There might be said a good deal about the erotic manifestations of the confusional Malay: I only will mention that very ·frank utterance is given to all his erotic thoughts, that however onanism is seen very seldom indeed. Perhaps a consequence of the absence of repression? (van Loon 1922:218).

Chance observations of colonial medical and administrative personnel, visitors and ethnographers do not constitute epidemiological data. Yet from such sources the accepted pronouncements are that: *latah* occurs primarily among Malays and there are higher frequency rates among women; those in subservient social positions are more vulnerable. Little substantive material or new data have been forthcoming, although various interpretations have been made.

Hildred Geertz, for example, has argued that *latah* is congruent with Javanese culture; the symptomatology is determined by cultural tradition and is 'unconsciously meaningful' as an inversion of Javanese cultural values and ideals of appropriate behaviour. She also asserts that Javanese women do not endure a subservient position or play a restricted role. Most Javanese women, including those who suffer *latah*, are self-confident and assertive (Geertz 1968:103). Pfeiffer on the other hand, reproduces a cultural stereotype - the submissive, inert torpid character of the Malay race in general and of the Malay woman in particular. He detected a parallel between the surrender and passivity of the *latah* state and his image of the Javanese woman (1968:37).

Rejecting the 'disease' model of *latah* and discounting possible bio-medical elements, Kenny (1978, 1983) defined *latah* as a cultural reaction to low status and social marginality and a means of overcoming them. Thus he perceived it as a 'putative mental disorder' rooted in Javanese metaphysical conceptions. Having rejected biological determinants in *latah,* Kenny argued that it was primarily theatre performance, dramatic mimesis or parody of social norms by lower status women; a kind of socially-sanctioned obscenity in contrast to culturally preferred refinement. Thus, he saw *latah* symptomatology as a 'peculiarly appropriate means of communicating... marginality to others' and a device whereby lower status and distress are acknowledged and surmounted (Kenny 1983:160.)

Murphy attempted a quasi-epidemiological study of both *latah* and *amok* in order to demonstrate his hypothesis that they are by-products of social problem-solving, tending to increase when the imperative for adaptive change was highest:

> ...*latah* appeared relatively suddenly during the second half of the nineteenth century, spread quite rapidly among the populations most exposed to European influence, and then moved in a wave fashion away from these centres, so that today it is virtually absent in the locations where it was first observed but is present in more distant locations where it was previously absent... and in areas from which it is disappearing the residual subjects seem less intelligent than the earlier ones (1972:47).

With a limited understanding of the phenomena, and on the basis of outsiders' fortuitous encounters with clinical cases, can we know anything significant concerning the incidence and prevalence of *latah* or of age and sex frequencies? Can we judge the whole from a limited knowledge of a small unrepresentative sample of the population? As Leighton has commented, the epidemiologic work on these disorders is weak to non-existent. Estimations of frequency are vague. When numbers are used they are 'numerators without denominators' (1982:217). The finding that there are high rates of mental disorder among the lower socio-economic levels of society may say more about the composition of the population than anything else. Moreover, the observers disagree (cf. Geertz 1958; Kenny 1983; Simons 1980).

Yet, among the various Asian populations in which culture-bound syndromes have been observed there is a marked similarity in symptomatology, a combination of non-neurological and neurological symptoms and signs. This symptomatology as described in case studies, together with that of *babainan* described in local medical sources, seems to me to indicate more a universal human neuropathological potential (cf. Sechrest 1969:329; Simons 1980) than conformity to a pattern of 'madness' resulting from cultural sanctions and predilections. That the syndromes occur among peoples with comparable technologies, who face similar forms of environmental stress, high rates of morbidity and low standards of hygiene could be vital analytical data. Yet, from the narrow perspective of psychodynamic formulations, one could gain the erroneous impression that among the populations of Southeast Asia there is an inordinate number of hysterical paranoid, neurotic hypochondriacal maniacs who are predisposed to a poor tolerance of anxiety, who tend to express their emotional tensions somatically and act out unresolved discontents through flights of aggressive passion, panic or fatuous euphoria (cf. Stoller 1969; Obeyesekere 1979).

Against views which deny a place to neurophysiology in the genesis and expression of *latah,* I would argue that *latah* behaviour, like the mental symptoms displayed in *babainan,* constitutes a radical departure from social norms and standards of etiquette in any culture. Admittedly, feigned or simulated insanity, mental or social distress might account for some cases of diagnosed *latah* and *babainan* but not for all the individuals so affected, or for the *babainan* syndrome itself as it is described in local medical treatises. Judgement, self-control and discernment are as highly valued in Asian societies as they are elsewhere. Loss of control or awareness and disorientation are not states to which people normally aspire. The notion of women taking recourse to bizarre behaviour indicative of mental derangement to improve their lot, does not even sound logical. Besides, what exactly are the afflicted supposed to gain from feigned derangement? Most are long term sufferers. They do not enjoy it. In fact, the afflicted suffer extreme discomfort and helplessness, according to Yap (1952:550). Moreover, the behavioural symptoms appear to relate to activities of the brain, and the *latah* predicament broaches as many (or more) problems for the sufferers as it could possibly resolve. If repressive social structures and interpersonal conflict (the salience of which is not doubted) were conducive to the genesis of culture-bound syndromes and their symptomatology, one might perhaps expect even higher incidences of them. I dare say many observed *latah* sufferers were experiencing problematic social relationships and stress at the time of affliction. Few people in any culture secure for themselves a stress-free existence.

(v) Models of Madness; Paradigms and Platitudes

The 'outlandish' races discovered through colonial penetrations became the objects of European efforts to define mental disturbance among 'more civilised races'. Thus Sigmund Freud wrote:

> Primitive man is known to us by the stages of development through which he has passed... and through remnants of his ways of thinking that survive in our own manners and customs. Moreover, in a certain sense he is still our contemporary: there are people whom we still consider more closely related to primitive man than to ourselves, in whom we therefore recognise the direct descendants and representatives of earlier man. We can thus judge the so-called savage and semi-savage races; their psychic life assumes a peculiar interest for us, for we can recognise in their psychic life a well-preserved, early stage of our own development (1938:15).

Freud posited correspondences between taboo customs and the symptoms of compulsive neurosis (1938:48). Decades later, analogies and comparisons using an evolutionary framework were still asserted, as the following statement from Yap indicates:

> We must finally mention an important psychiatric generalisation which affirms that there is an analogy between schizophrenic and primitive ways of thought... the *analogy* between primitive savage thinking and the regressed schizophrenic thinking is often striking (1951:324).

Both psychiatric and a significant proportion of anthropological research in Asia was initiated for the purpose of studying cultural influences on the frequency and symptomatology of mental disorders. In some quarters the physical and biochemical differences between population groups, used as criteria for racial classifications, came to be regarded as having psychological implications and intellectual and behavioural correspondences. For example, anthropological research on Bali conducted by Bateson, Mead and Belo was initiated by a request from the Committee for the Study of Dementia Praecox (now called schizophrenia) for a cultural study which could lead to a better understanding of the condition. A reconnaisance of Balinese mental health was also part of the objective. The choice of Bali for this comparative study was determined by the presupposition that the culture was one in which a significant percentage of the population, while exhibiting many of the overt behavioural characteristics and 'test responses' associated with schizophrenia in Western cultures, were able to lead normal lives and function within the dissociated mode of functioning expected in that society (cf. Belo 1970; Bateson 1970; Mead 1970, 1979).

These researchers maintained that, in the study of Balinese trance and ritual, they had encountered thought processes of the same order as those which psychoanalysts had described in schizophrenics and likened to primitive archaic thought. Beklo (1970) applied performance tests to trance mediums in order to see if the tendency to think in 'complexes' characteristic of schizophrenics, was also a tendency among Balinese trance subjects. Mead and Bateson described psychopathological tendencies, posited cultural, child-rearing and socialisation techniques (such as teasing and withdrawing) as causal factors in psychogenesis, designating them as standard forms of emotional release or repressed aggression (Mead 1970, 1979; Bateson 1970).

Mental illness has captured the imagination of those for whom the poignancy and spectacle of clinical manifestations of dysfunction of the nervous system are no longer a conspicuous part of their pattern of morbidity. Indeed, madness has been assigned a peculiar status by the Western social scientific industry: as Derrida comments, Foucault aspires to capture 'untamed madness'... 'in its most vibrant state' rejecting bio-medical data in favour of popular notions from unverifiable sources (Derrida 1981:34).

In a critique of Freud and trends in psychoanalytical theory, Brewer suggests an alarmingly simple reason for the preeminence of psychodynamic theories and the non-assertiveness of the neuropathologic view:

> The phrase 'the devil has all the best tunes' was surely created with Freud and his disciples in mind. Who could hope to compete with penis envy, castration anxiety... (1982:685).

and, I would add, with catchy cliches like Laing's 'the blessed mad with special insight', 'culturally-sanctioned escape-hatches for the repressed', or 'flight into illness'. For those who choose to reject a bio-medical paradigm in the study of mental illness, variations on the Laingian credo - do not adjust your brain, there is something wrong with your racial, mental endowment, your culture or your society's philosophical assumptions - legitimate this stance. Does the conspiracy implicit in the trend of the 1960s that 'the brain, uniquely among all organs, does not go wrong' (Brewer 1982:686) remain?

Encapsulated within a metaphysical aetiology, the Balinese do have a medical model of madness. Neurological and non-neurological diseases share similar aetiological options and metaphysical and pathological mechanisms. Impairment of the faculties of intellect and judgement, loss of control, inability to differentiate the appropriateness of behaviour and speech (madness and insanity in latter-day terminology) are locally defined as abnormal and of the same order as somatic symptoms of disease. Such symptomatology is generically labelled *edan* and *buduh*. It may occur as a phase of other generic categories (e.g. of *tuju* or *tiwang*) or in the febrile phase of any illness. All abnormality, whether primarily affecting the physical component of the body or mind, is termed illness (*gering*). Balinese concepts of mental disturbance share a perspective found in classical Ayurvedic theory wherein mental derangement is explained without any reference whatsoever to psychodynamic theory (cf. Obeysekere 1977:161). The intrusion of pathological agents (however they are perceived) is the basis of disordered mental function. *Edan* (or *buduh*) is a potential phase in any dynamic morbid process and it is dominant in some forms of disease. While there is no obvious description of mental derangement due to brain lesions, there is a theory of pathogens (be they a *babai* or those responsible for *tiwang*, for example) moving to the head, the location of mind, language ability, perception and cognition, and precipitating disturbance and disorganisation.

Balinese medical theory does not have a category of mental disorders of a psychogenic origin corresponding to neurosis, phobia, hysteria, paranoia, fear psychosis and hypochondriasis. States of fear, anxiety, depression and agitation are normal reactions to life's stresses. Prolonged exacerbation of these natural states for no apparent reason are not labelled deviant or abnormal psychological reactions. On the mind-body issue, Balinese medical theory shares the neurologist's position of psychophysical monism. There is no mind/ body dichotomy. In Balinese medical theory, the mind is an inseparable part of the living organism. It does not exist independently of the body (or act against it). The soul is another matter.

Madness *(edan)* can afflict any group, including infants, a matter which should undermine the notion of psychosocial origins of mental symptoms like fright, listlessness or abnormal grasping and groping. Of course the range of abnormality of affective, perceptive and cognitive experience an infant can express is limited. The point being made is that Balinese medical theory does not differentiate linguistically or conceptually between 'madness' expressed in a person running berserk, displaying aphasia or other forms of behaviour characteristic of culture-bound syndromes, and blurred consciousness or loss of consciousness which are clearly indicative of neuropathological defined disease.

I am not arguing that nature, in the sense of neuropathology, is an exclusive alternative to socio-cultural factors in explanation. Obviously, specific behaviour patterns, life-styles and ritual practices influence the content of symptomatology and, to some extent, account for the degree of conformity displayed in the syndromes. An individual sustaining a grave assault to the central nervous system in an urban Western society is unlikely to scramble up a tree to evade would-be captors, to flourish a kris or to hallucinate the fantastic images peculiar to the Balinese visual landscape and iconography. Indeed, the vocabulary of madness does have a strong cultural content. The abnormality of such behaviour is defined only by the inappropriateness, undirectedness or excessiveness of the activity. To run amok and stab one's opponents and finally oneself on a battlefield is not classified as madness. To run amok as an individual without any apparent cause is abnormality indicative of pathology. When Javanese and Balinese act with undirected, unprovoked hostility and run amok, they often do so with a kris. However, the form of this disorganisation pertains to brain activity. Because the symptomatology of mental disorder is expressed in a cultural idiom and reflects metaphysical assumptions, the condition is not explicable simply in cultural terms (cf. Leighton 1982:219-20). Such an explanation draws attention away from the actuality of disease problems facing peoples of Asia and focuses upon the imputed proclivity of 'culture-types' to express dissatisfaction and aggression through feigned affliction, and to somatize mental distress. Notwithstanding the cultural elaborations woven around *babainan,* the syndrome itself is not simply a product of culture. Disease is mediated through a system of symbols (call it culture) but the nature of the pathogen directs the form which cultural representations (the symbolism) take. This is the reason why *babainan* is constructed differently in Bali from, say, smallpox or leprosy.

What also needs to be addressed are the politics of medical research which are directed largely towards the artificial prolongation of the lives of the more affluent while diseases afflicting the mass of the world's population thrive. Too much emphasis on the role of culture and the imputed psychosocial tendencies of Third World population groups, whose diseases present with mental symptoms, shirks consideration of the ecology of poverty and of survival in a harsh tropical and unsanitary environment. The human neurological system is particularly susceptible to damage from nutritional deficiencies and to infections that are rife in such an environment. There is accumulating evidence that foetal and infantile malnutrition, anaemia (resulting from parasitic infections) and catastrophic infections associated with febrile convulsions have a deleterious effect upon the developing brain that time does not heal. Acute and chronic infections can present with behavioural disturbances when lesions occur in the frontal lobes of the brain. Vitamin deficiencies and malnutrition can present as acute organic psychoses. Infection-induced psychoses are also likely to be more prominent in tropical Southeast Asia than in temperate regions (Orley and Tsuang 1983:24-48). Most infectious diseases interfere with the body's intake of food and capacity to absorb it. Malnutrition then lowers resistance to infections. Although genetic susceptibility may also be pertinent, nutritional deficiency has contributed to various (obscure) neuropathies. The notion of a 'lethal synthesis', for example, in people suffering malaria, parasitic disease, infections and malnutrition, could be relevant to the aetiology of the not-yet-understood phenomena that are the subject matter of this paper.

It is suggested that because Western observers described certain 'bizarre' (unfamiliar) syndromes among 'exotic' (other) Asian populations, there was little inhibition to their constructing a set of 'atypical reactive psychoses' which made sense to Western psychiatric nosology'; associated exotica were then attributed first to racial personality and intelligence and later to 'culture personality'.

Accounts of culture-bound syndromes such as *latah* are worthy of a study in their own right insofar as they reveal a shift from the renounced racial-determinist arguments to cultural-determinist ones wherein the content of the imputed contributing factors remain basically unchanged. In the first, there is a racial type in a 'lower' evolutionary stage of psychical development and vulnerable to 'imbecility' and 'primitive reactions' in the presence of 'more cultured races'. In the second, there is a 'cultural personality' predisposed to feigning forms of madness in order to cope with crises and repression. Anthropological research in this area in particular highlights the nurture-over-nature triumph to which Freeman (1983) refers. Culture, that 'common-sense' factor in human experience (cf. Geertz 1983), is allegedly maladaptive, even pathogenic.

My argument is that this produces cultural stereotyping along the lines once rightly condemned as racial stereotyping. The same data have been used to draw conclusions which reflect the disciplinary interests and commitments of the particular researcher, as well as the changing aetiologic view - culture not race - of Western academic enterprise. This has meant little expansion in knowledge of Asian medical problems or experience. Granted the present state of our knowledge of tropical neurology, the use of the phrase culture-bound syndrome, in the acquired sense of culture-induced, seems to me racist and prejudicial to Asian populations, even if unintentionally so.

Although a consideration of the effects of culture, in the sense of customs of life-style, on the transmission of disease may be justified, there is good reason to be cautious with formulations which arraign culture as causative,

127

at least until further studies of tropical neurology have been undertaken and local medical knowledge has been examined.

Bibliography

Kawi Manuscripts

HKS   Hooykaas-ketut Sangka Proyek Tik. These are listed according to the numbers assigned to manuscripts by Proyek Tik.

K   Gedong Kirtya Collection

Pangalah Babai	HSK3124
Pangalah Babai	K269
Paribhasa	K173
Tingkah ing Babahi	HKS 47, 25
Tingkah ing Ngubah Babahi	HKS2183
Usada Babai	HKS3741
Usada Buduh	HKS1113, 7
Usada Edan	HKS3558
Usada Sasah	K422
Usada Tuju Dest Babahi	HKS3097

Annual Reports of the Netherlands Indies Public Health Service 1934-1939, MDVG. *Bali Post* (Newspaper 22.10.76. [Baru 1, 2 pCt Raykat Indonesia Yg Pernah Dilayani Dokter].

Bateson, Gregory (1970) 'Bali: The Value System of a Steady State', in Belo (1970): 384-401.

Bateson, Gregory & Margaret Mead (1942) *Balinese Character; A Photographic Analysis* New York, Academy of Sciences XVI.

Belo, Jane (1970) *Traditional Balinese Culture* New York, Columbia University Press.

Brewer, Colin (1982) 'The Yellow-brick Road to Happiness' *New Scientist*, 95(1322):684-86.

Brown, Jann & Marietta Voge (1982) *Neuropathology of Parasitic Infections*, Oxford University Press.

Caudill, William & Tsung-Yi Lin (1969) *Mental Health Research in Asia and the Pacific* Honolulu, East-West Center Press.

Connor, Linda H. (1979) 'Corpse Abuse and Trance in Bali: The Cultural Mechanism of Aggression' *Mankind* 12:104-18.

----- (1982) 'Ships of Fools and Vessles of the Divine: Mental Hospitals and Madness, A Case Study' *Social Science and Medicine* 16:783-94.

Derrida, Jacques (1981) *Writing and Difference*. Alan Bass (trans.) London: Routledge and Kegan Paul.

Edington, G.M. & H.M. Gilles (1976) *Pathology in the Tropics*, London, Edward Arnold.

Ellard, John (1985) 'The Anatomy of Mirages' *Modern Medicine of Australia* 28(2):17-19.

Endicott, Kirk Michael (1970) *An Analysis of Malay Magic* Oxford, Clarendon Press.

Fabrega, Horacio (1977) 'On the Specificity of Folk Illnesses' in Landy, (1977) pp.273-8.

Fitzgerald, R.D. (1923) A Thesis on Two Tropical Neuroses (Amok and Latah) Peculiar to Malaya *Transactions of the Fifth Congress, FEATM* (Far Eastern Association of Tropical Medicine), Singapore, pp.148-61.

Foucault, Michel (1979) *Madness and Civilisation; A History of Insanity in the Age of Reason* London, Tavistock Publications.

Freeman, Derek (1983) *Margaret Mead and Samoa, The Making and Unmaking of an Anthropological Myth* Harvard University Press.

Freud, Sigmund (1938) *Totem and Taboo; Resemblances Between the Psychic Lives and Savages and Neurotics* Harmondsworth, Penguin.

Galloway, Sir David J. (1923) 'On Amok' in *Transactions of the Fifth Congress FEATM.* Singapore, pp.162-71.

Gaydusek, D.C. (1973) 'Kuru in the New Guinea Highlands' in Spillane (1973) pp.376-83.

Geertz, Clifford (1983) *Local Knowledge; Further Essays in Interpretive Anthropology* New York, Basic Books, Inc.

Geertz, Hildred (1968) 'Latah in Java. A Theoretical Paradox' *Indonesia* 5:93-104.

Gimlette, J.D. (1923) *Malay Poisons and Charm Cures* London, J. and A. Churchill.

Kenny, Michael G. (1978) 'Latah: The Symbolism of a Putative Mental Disorder' *Culture, Medicine and Psychiatry* 2:209-32.

----- (1983) 'Paradox Lost: The Latah Problem Revisited' *Journal of Nervous and Mental Disease* 17(3):159-67.

Kleinman, Arthur (1980) *Patients and Healers in the Context of Culture; An Exploration of the Borderland between Anthropology, Medicine and Psychiatry* Berkeley, University of California Press.

Landy, David (ed.) (1977) *Culture, Diseases and Healing* New York, Macmillan.

Leff, Julia (1981) *Psychiatry Around the Glove* New York, Marcel Dekker Inc.

Leighton, Alexander H. (1969) 'Cultural Relativity and the Identification of Psychiatric Disorders' in Caudill & Tsung-Yi (1969) pp.448-62.

----- (1982) 'Relevant Generic Issues' in Albert Gaw (ed.) *Cross-Cultural Psychiatry* Boston, John Wright PSG Inc., pp.199-236.

Lishman, William Alwyn (1980) 'The Problem of Lunacy in Acheen' *MBGD* X:2-49.

----- (1922) 'Acute Confusional Insanity in the Dutch East Indies' *MBGD* IV:200-20.

----- (1924) 'Latah, A Psycho-Neurosis of the Malay Races' *MBGD* III:305-20.

Lovric, B.J.A. (1979) An Approach to Balinese Historical Literature BA (Hons) Thesis, University of Sydney.

----- (1987a) Bali; Myth, Magic and Morbidity in Norman Owen (ed.) , 1987, pp117-41.

----- (1987b) Rhetoric and Reality: The Hidden Nightmare. PhD thesis, University of Sydney.

Maegraith, Brian (1984) *Adams & MMaegraith; Clinical Tropical Diseases* Oxford, Blackwell Scientific Publications.

Mead, Margaret (1970) [1939] *'The Strolling Players in the Mountains of Bali', in Belo (1970) pp. 137-45.*

----- *(1970)* [1955] *'Children and Ritual in Bali', in Belo (1970) pp.198-211.*

----- *(1970)* [1940] *The Arts in Bali, in Belo, J. (op.cit.) 1970, pp.331-40.*

----- *(1979) Letters from the Field 1925-1975 New York, Harper Colophon Books.*

Meededeelingen van den Burgerlijken Geneeskundigen Dienst in Nederlandsch-Indie (MBGD), Batavia, 1913-1925.

Mededeelingen van den Dienst der Volksgezondheid in Nederlandsch-Indie (MDVG), Batavia, 1926-1941.

Murphy, H.B.M. (1972) 'History and the Evolution of Syndromes: The Striking Case of Latah and Amok', in M. Hammer et al., (eds), *Psychopathology; Contributions from the Social, Behavioural, and Biological Sciences* New York, John Wiley & Sons, pp.33-55.

----- (1978) Abstract and Review of Michael G. Kenny's 'Latah: The Symbolism' and John E. Carr's 'Ethno-Behaviourism and the Culture-bound Syndromes: The Case of Amok', *Transcultural Psychiatric Research 16;61-64.*

Obeysekere, Gananath (1970) The Idiom of Demonic Possession. *Social Science in Medicine* 4:97-111.

----- (1975) 'Psychocultural Exegesis of a Case of Spirit Possession in Sri Lanka' *Contributions to Asian Studies* 8:41-89.

----- (1977) 'The Theory and Practice of Psychological Medicine in the Auyrvedic Tradition' *Culture, Medicine and Psychiatry* 1(2):155-81.

Orley, J. & M.T. Tsuang (1983) 'Psychiatry and Medicine in the Developing Countries', in Weatherall et al., (1983) Vol.II, 24:47-8.

Owen, Norman (ed) (1987) *Death and Disease in South East Asia*, Singapore, Oxford Univ. Press for Asian Studies Association of Australia.

Peters, Sir Rudolph A. (1963) *Biochemical Lesions and Lethal Synthesis* Oxford, Pergamon Press.

Pfeiffer, W. (1968) 'New Research Findings Regarding Latah' *Transcultural Psychiatric Research.* 5:34-38.

Samuels, W.F. (1923) 'Malaria and Mental Disease' *Transactions of the Fifth Congress FEATM*, Singapore, pp.141-7.

Sechrest, Lee (1969) 'Philippine Culture, Stress and Psychopathology', in Caudill and Tsung-Yi Lin (1969) pp. 306-34.

Simons, Ronald C. (1980) 'The Resolution of the Latah Paradox' *The Journal of Nervous and Mental Disease* 168(4):195-206.

Spillane, John D. (ed.) (1973) *Tropical Neurology* London, Oxford University Press.

----- (1974) 'Neurology in the Tropics. Proceedings of the Tenth International Congress of Neurology. Barcelona, 1973, in A. Subirana and J.M. Espadaler (eds.) *Neurology* New York, Elsevier Publishing Co. Inc., pp.265-72.

Stoller, Alan (1969) 'Parameters of Mental Illness and Mental Health: A Public Health Approach', in Caudill and Tsung-Yi Lin (1969) pp.3-20.

Surya, N.C. (1969) 'Ego Structure in the Hindu Joint Family: Some Considerations', in Caudill and Tsung-Yi Lin (1969) pp.381-92.

Taori, G.M. & G.V. Iyer (1973) 'Neurological Complications in Tropical Sprue', in Spillane (1973) pp.73-7.

Theunissen, W.F. (1921) 'A Contribution to the Knowledge of the Indian Psychoses' *Transactions of the Fourth Congress FEATM* Batavia, pp.78-89.

Torpin, Richard (1968) *Fetal Malformations Caused by Amnion Rupture During Gestation* Springfield Illinois, Charles C. Thomas.

Travaglino, P.H.M. (1920) 'The Psychosis of the Native in Relation to His Character' *MBGD* II:38-49.

Trimble, Michael R. (1981) *Neuropsychiatry* New York, John Wiley and Sons.

Wadia, N.H. (1973) 'An Introduction to Neurology in India', in Spillane, (1973) pp.25-36.

Warren, Kenneth S. & Adel A.F. Mahmoud (1984) *Tropical and Geographical Medicine* New York, McGraw-Hill Book Company.

Weatherall, D.J. et al. (1983) *Oxford Textbook of Medicine* Vols I and II Oxford University Press.

Weck, Wolfgang (1973) *Heilkunde und Volkstum auf Bali* Stuttgart, Ferdinand Enke.

Weidman, Hazel Hitson (1969) Abstract and Review of John G. Kennedy's 'Psychosocial Dynamics of Witchcraft Systems' *Transcultural Psychiatric Research VI;116-%.*

Winzeler, Robert (1984) 'The Study of Malayan Latah' Indonesia 37:77-104.

Wittkower, Eric D. & P.E. Termanson (1969) 'Cultural Psychiatric Research in Asia', in Caudill and Tsung-Yi (1969) pp.433-37.

Yap, P.M. (1951) 'Mental Diseases Peculiar to Certain Cultures: A Survey of Comparative Psychiatry' *Journal of Mental Science* 97-313-28.

----- (1952) 'The Latah Reaction: Its Pathodynamics and Nosological Position' *Journal of Mental Science* 98:515-64.

----- (1967) 'Classification of the Culture-Bound Reactive Syndromes' *Australian and New Zealand Journal of Psychiatry*, 1:172-9.

----- (1969) 'The Culture-Bound Reactive Syndromes,' in Caudill and Tsung-Yi Lind (1969) pp.33-53.

'My Struggle': The Congealing of History

Phil Barker

Whatever our theoretical differences might be within the Academy, and they seem quite considerable, we all seem to be sure that racism - as discourse and political practice - takes place, and was taking place, outside, outside our discourse. So it appears that we have constructed an outside for our theoretical practice. An outside that allows us to occupy, even colonise, the inside which is also the true-side and, one might be tempted to say, the rightside, the side of the moral high ground of racist discourse. This paper attempts to collapse these distinctions through the vehicle of the philosophy of history.

My contribution here places before you another discourse, among the discourses about discourses, that looks at the question of identity, from within a conception of the philosophy of history. Or to put it rather less coyly and less sensitively, this paper is both about, and in some sense represents, one kind of struggle for identity, for a name and for a place within discourse.

Of course to struggle with one's writing is a common theme to all the humanities and in particular to philosophy. One could offer many illustrious examples of such struggles, from Augustine's *Confessions* to Abelard's *Historia Calamitatum*, and to Hegel's *Phenomenology of Spirit*. These texts besides all being certain kinds of struggles have an intimate relation with the dual modes of biography and autobiography (cf. Barker, 1985), but for now I want to stress that there is a certain kind of literary/ philosophical history to be taken into account here, a history where the struggle with a text has become an essential part of the history of philosophy. This brings me to the point where I want to direct attention to one of those great philosophical struggles that has somehow escaped classification as philosophical; this text goes by the name of 'My Struggle', although its title is almost never translated into English even when the rest of the text is, and so we nearly all know it still in its German title as *Mein Kampf* (Hitler, 1983). The untranslatability of this title is perhaps a mark of the demonic nature of the text itself, a sign that this is the product of a culture alien to the English speaking world, a culture that traces its origins back to the Visigoths or Huns who, according to popular English history, were the descendants of non Greek speaking barbarians who had been causing trouble in Europe for thousands of years and who were ultimately responsible for the decline of the high culture of the Roman empire. This might all be seen as the nonsense for which it obviously is, were it not for the fact that the question of the untranslatability of *Mein Kampf* is suspended by the intervention of a publisher's note inside the front cover of the 1983 text before the translator, the writer or the authorised introducer have been given any opportunity to speak. I quote:

> This notorious book did not circulate in this country or in the Commonwealth territories for many years-in fact from 1944-1969 when this edition, in hard bound format, was published mainly for public library use, with the valuable introduction by D.C. Watt. It is now thought right that a rather less expensive edition in paper binding should also be available for students and others who need reminding of the vile nonsense which precipitated World War II and which has become for ever a fact of history... The origin of Hitler is almost irrelevant. What is important is that he existed, that he brought tragedy to his people and the world, and that there are still sympathisers in many parts of the world today. *Mein Kampf* is a compendium of their prejudices and ignorance, whether they belong to the German, British or any other nation.
>
> It is therefore necessary that Hitler, their prototype, 'the master of the inept, the undigested, the half baked and the untrue', should be understood. *Mein Kampf* is an introduction to his mind and methods, and as such should be readily available for study by all and, in our view, in every language.
>
> In his Introduction Professor Watt sets Hitler against his background, gives the origins and history of *Mein Kampf* and finishes with a critical assessment of the book. This book will alas continue for ever to be essential reading for all students of twentieth-century history. It cannot be ever forgotten that millions had to die to rid the world of the evil creed it so violently imposed. (Hitler, 1983 inside front cover).

D.C. Watt the introducer goes on to refer to Hitler as a demon, and speaks of *Mein Kampf* in terms of the 'peculiar illiteracy of its contribution to political literature', and then talks of its origins. The unconscious reference to the demonic with its double meaning of both evil and genius, and the absence of this text for fifteen years from English publication, perhaps has something to do with its suggestive power for a European culture to become increasingly fascist. At the very least, we can say that if we characterise *Mein Kampf* as mad or even demonic then we can see it as an aberration, a detour from the 'progressive' civilising influence of Western culture. This seems to me to be all rather too easy, because like it or not *Mein Kampf* is part of the cultural heritage of the West and rather than dismiss it out of hand we might do better perhaps to subject it to the kind of analysis to which other philosophical and literary texts are subjected. We might then discover something rather more frightening, that *Mein Kampf* is neither demonic nor mad but a necessary event within the culture of the West. Fascism and its accompanying racism would then equally not be mad or demonic but part of that same history, and this is surely rather more disturbing than a fascism and a racism of madness, darkness and barbarism.

Before pausing to pick up the themes from *Mein Kampf* that I want to discuss, a question needs reiterating. Why is it that *Mein Kampf* is excluded from its rightful textual place in the history of philosophy? For without a doubt, in *Mein Kampf* and other writings by Hitler a number of the themes dealt with and references given come directly from the history of philosophy, as it had been conceived by academics working in Europe after the first world war. So we find mention of Fichte, Schopenhauer, Voltaire, Rousseau, Goethe, Luther, Wagner, Schiller and others. The theme of the relation between philosophy, desire and death, so central in *Mein Kampf* has its own discontinuous philosophical history from Socrates to Abelard to Rousseau, de Sade and so on. The question then is why is this text not considered to be part of the history or philosophy? I do not propose to offer an answer here, but the question is worth raising.

What I want to draw out of *Mein Kampf* is a theme repeated over and over again in the writings of Hitler, namely, the attaining of a personal identity by overcoming namelessness. I do not propose here to develop an argument that psychoanalyses Hitler's relation with his father, although such a paper could no doubt prove interesting, but the theme of personal identity, namelessness and its overcoming does provide the thread that this paper will attempt to follow.

In a speech in Dusseldorf in 1932 Hitler said about his return from the war in 1918:

> I was naturally forced to say to myself that it would be an appalling struggle, for I was not so fortunate to possess an outstanding name; I was only a nameless German soldier, with a small zinc identification number on my breast (Hitler, 1942:95).

In 1939, he reiterated this preoccupation:

> Twenty years ago, nameless and alone, I began. Nineteen years ago I stood for the first time in this place, facing alone a shouting mob, many of whom still opposed me. (Hitler, 1942:474).

Again, in 1940, he returned to this theme:

> Who was I before the Great War? An unknown nameless individual.

What was I during the war? A quite inconspicuous ordinary soldier... Should anyone say to me: 'These are more fantastic dreams, mere visions', I can only reply that when I set out on my course in 1919 as an unknown nameless soldier I built my hopes of the future upon a most vivid imagination. Yet all has come true. What I am planning or aiming at today is nothing compared to what I have already accomplished and achieved. It will be achieved sooner and more definitely than everything already achieved. The road from an unknown and nameless person to Führer of the German nation was harder than the way from the Führer of the German nation to creator of the coming peace. (Hitler, 1942:709,716).

And then perhaps most significantly of all we learn in *Mein Kampf* of the founding instance of the Nazi party,

> Consider that six or seven men, all nameless poor devils, had joined together with the intention of forming a mass movement, hoping to succeed - where the powerful great mass of parties had hitherto failed - in restoring a German Reich of greater power and glory. (Hitler, 1983;353).

I apologise for quoting so much here but it seems to me that there is an important point to be made, that is, the search for a name, for an identity, the need to make something of oneself, is a constitutive element of fascism. This certainly is not so foreign to those of us who work within the Academy, as to a large extent one's success here is also dependent on making a name for ourselves within our chosen fields. I say this not to suggest that we must therefore all be fascists, but to remind us that the issues raised in this paper are perhaps not so far away from us as we might like to think.

To this something else must be added, something that emerges from the last quote, the claim to an identity is also based on a certain conception of one's cultural history, found in the return to the glorious past. So a personal history and a cultural history fuse together to produce something that we might call fascist micro-techniques of desire. These cultural and personal histories intersect in a certain kind of historical methodology that is discussed and examined by Foucault in the essay *Nietzsche, Genealogy and History?* (Foucault, 1980:139-164).

The return to the glorious past, to the achievements of a golden age, is the kind of history described by Foucault as the search for origins, which corresponds to a distinction made by Nietzsche in the Preface to the *Genealogy of Morals* between *Herkunft* and *Ursprung* (Nietzsche, 1969). Foucault interprets *Ursprung* as the search for origins, embodying the earlier Nietzschean terms of Antiquarian, Monumental and Objective History; and *Herkunft* he interprets as Critical History which he will recast and transform as Genealogy (cf. Nietzsche, 1983:57-124; Foucault, 1980;

Barker, 1985). Foucault argues that there are three problems with the search for origins which I paraphrase below;

1) It is an attempt to capture the essence of things, their past purest moments, which implies that at the end of it all lies some pure immobile form underlying a world of chance or coincidental effects. It appeals to some primordial truth, some original true identity under a series of masks.

2) The moment of origin is a metaphysical concept derived from the idea that things are 'most' precious and essential at the moment of their birth. That 'once upon a time', things were perfectly clear, good, and everything was known, then came the fall - time, space and history.

3) Which is a combination of 1) and 2) is that 'the postulate of the origin' is ultimately the site of truth. The origin becomes the place of loss, where the truth of 'things' corresponds to the truthful discourse - the sight of 'a fleeting articulation that discourse has obscured and finally lost'.

And to this might be added a fourth point derived from Foucault's other writings,

4) The construction of history as a unity, marked by an unfolding temporality becomes the founding instance of subjectivity within Western culture. Whether this subject is Rationalist, Dialectical, Positivist and so on, it is parasitic on specific notions of continuity, temporality, truth and transparency etc.

The plea in *Mein Kampf* for the return to a glorious past, to an age of golden dreams, finds a double leverage as this past becomes that moment of pure unadulterated heroic Aryan blood. This then is the intersection of both the glorious state and the pure blood of the race that occupied it; both must be returned to, recaptured and re-experienced. Every detail must be made known, made clear, from the unbroken history of an age old Aryan culture to the infinitesimal micro details of the distribution of the cells of that pure blood that transmits both that history and subjectivity on to the present day.

This process becomes the congealing of history, whereby history can be added to, altered, rewritten as long as the basic assumptions of the return to origins and its attendant continuities and unities are not challenged. This congealing of history and the tracing of the uncontaminated pure blood become in effect the same metaphor. A pure moment of the unfolding of absolute history, unadulterated, uncontaminated, disease free, frozen, against which individual identity and subjectivity are measured.

This absolute history is the history against which the individual finds a space in the social structure; the defining of the origin becomes the overcoming of namelessness, a history and a place is offered from which to claim an identity. All those who cannot or will not share in this history, this blood, become the absolute other, the bearers of disease and contamination, the evil against which good or self interest can be measured.

To recapitulate then, two themes that we can draw out of *Mein Kampf* are the desire to overcome namelessness and the recovery of an origin in which is located one's glorious cultural history. Of course, because they are both elements of fascism it does not mean that this is the only site of their expression. We must now look closer to home because in bicentennial Australia the conjunction of these two elements is again coming to the fore. This is occurring in a double instance: first, in the recovery of the so-called finally truthful Anglo-European Australian historical past, and secondly, in the re-representation of Aboriginal culture from eons ago to its interaction with Northern European culture. What these seemingly antithetical programmes have in common is that they both re-enact the search for origins, the origin of contemporary Australian culture, the origin of white settlement, the origin of Aboriginal culture and even on occasions, at least in the fairly recent past, the origin of universal man. Parallel with this is the production of a host of positive identities that fulfil the role of overcoming namelessness, and offer a secure identity, a home, and a foundational history from which to live and die.

Both projects rely on the production of unities, continuities, and an unfolding temporal sequence that stretches back countless thousands of years, to 1788, and up to the present day. Numerous points along this historical chain are being filled in, every detail is being made known, as a definitive Australian bloodline is being constructed and defined against the restoring of the origin. But there is I think an intuition developing that 'something else is going on', something rather subtle, because no matter who is speaking, from where and to whom, there is a suspicion that in the search for origins, and the overcoming of namelessness, there are transmitted specific conceptions of subjectivity that are derived from the history of Western philosophy, a history that spans the nodal points of Descartes, Locke and Hegel but which is bridged by continuities, unities, and unfolding temporality and transparency.

The questions that emerge are: where does that leave us now; must we all simply acknowledge that in our theorising we are committed to certain fascist techniques? I do not think this is so. The issue here is, rather, that we might want to examine the use of the great theoretical unities, continuities, temporalities and transparencies, and trace their history, the kinds of relations they allow, and perhaps see if it is possible to develop alternative techniques for our analysis. Until now, I have been strategically looking at part of the history of these themes and their possible interrelations, and once again it is important to stress that while they are constitutive elements of fascism, it does not necessarily mean that to use them is to be a fascist, but it is necessary that the theoretical issues they raise are addressed.

So at this point I want to return again to the work of Michel Foucault because, in contrast to his description of the search for origins, he suggests as an alternative a history of descent which he renames genealogy. Foucault argues that the analysis of descent or genealogy is the history of articulating the differences and the disunities that underly the disassociation of self. So 'descent' does not go back in time in an attempt to retrace an unbroken continuity up to the present, but rather disperses history into discontinuous events. As Foucault says:

> ...it is to identify the accidents, the minute deviations - or conversely, the complete reversals - the errors, the false appraisals, and the faulty calculations that gave birth to those things that continue to exist and have value for us; it is to discover that truth or being do not lie at the root of what we know and what we are, but the exteriority of accidents (1980:142).

The object of the genealogical analysis is more often than not the body and everything that comes into contact with it - diet, soil, climate and so on - as the body is itself an inscribed surface of events, and the place of both the disassociation of subjectivity and the disintegration of its own bodily volume. So both the body and the self are not outside history; on the contrary they are the very condition of history as it is history that articulates specific selves and specific bodies; and genealogical history indicates an awareness of this and then makes it the basis of its method.

> Genealogy, as an analysis of descent, is thus situated within the articulation of the body and history. Its task is to expose a body totally imprinted by history's destruction of the body (Foucault, 1980:148).

Finally, Foucault develops the concept of 'emergence' as an instance of arising, not a continuous arising but a momentary instance, not the end of historical development but a transition between points that emerge momentarily from within the play of dominations and subjections. So genealogy and the history of descent do not seek origins, do not offer ultimate meanings, nor continuities, but only trace the play of dominations. Genealogy

> seeks to reestablish the various systems of subjection: not the anticipatory power of meaning, but the hazardous play of dominations (Foucault, 1980:148).

Foucault brings together the various elements of genealogy under the sign of 'effective' history: history that is without reference to any absolute, universal or constant, and from which not even the body or subjectivity escapes:

> History becomes 'effective' to the degree that it introduces discontinuity into our very being - as it divides our emotions, dramatises our instincts, multiplies our body and sets it against itself. 'Effective' history deprives the self of the reassuring stability of life and nature, and it will not permit itself to be transported by a voiceless obstinacy towards its millenial ending. It will uproot its traditional foundations and relentlessly disrupt its pretended continuity. This is because knowledge is not made for understanding; it is made for cutting (Foucault, 1980:154).

'Effective history' is the history of dispersal, of events, disruptions and discontinuity. It is a history of chance, random events and the analysis of the microcosm, the body, the nervous system; but above all it is a history that revels in its multi-perspectivism. It is a history that acknowledges the perspectivism of the historian's own path of descent. This is exactly what non-effective, non-genealogical history refuses to do. Under the various masks of universal subjectivity, truth, essences, objectivity and facts, social historians deny the specificity of their own bodily existence, their subjectivity and will, in order to uncover the abstract eternal will of history itself which is ultimately reduced to a final cause - Providence, Telos, Progressiveness, or some final absolute meaning and identity.

In drawing this paper to a close I want to restate a couple of points. It is absolutely crucial that a text like *Mein Kampf* is not allowed to remain silent today. We must subject it to detailed analysis if we are ever to come to terms with its themes of racism and fascism. But this coming to terms can only take place if fascism is seen not as a temporary deviance from the 'civilising progression' of Western culture, but as an essential part of the very conception of this 'progression', which we can reconstruct and theorise. But more than this we must analyse our own theoretical methodology. This paper is an attempt to achieve these two aims; perhaps a rather better one is the book *Anti-Oedipus* by Deleuze and Guattari (1977), but it is also very much longer.

Bibliography

Barker, P. (1985) 'On Foucault and History' *On the Beach,* 7/8, Summer-Autumn.
Deleuze, G. & Guattari, F. (1977) *Anti-Oedipus; Capitalism and Schizophrenia,* New York, Viking Press.
Foucault, M. (1980) *Language, Counter-Memory, Practice* Cornell University Press.
Hitler, A. (1942) *My New Order,* Sydney, Angus & Robertson.
Hitler, A. (1983) *Mein Kampf,* London, Hutchinson.
Nietzsche, F. (1969) *On the Genealogy of Morals* and *Ecce Homo,* New York, Vintage Books.
Nietzsche, F. (1983) *Untimely Meditations* Cambridge University Press.

SYDNEY ASSOCIATION FOR STUDIES
IN SOCIETY AND CULTURE
University of Sydney NSW 2006

SASSC is an interdisciplinary association which brings together scholars from all the human social sciences.

Our aims are:

- to provide a forum for work in areas which are marginalised or even excluded by existing departmental boundaries;

- to encourage ways of talking about social and cultural phenomena which the traditional disciplines do not allow;

- to publish and disseminate work in these areas which are not adequately covered in existing journals or by existing publishers;

- to bridge the gap between the human social sciences and the physical and life sciences.

To further these aims we hold conferences and workshops for scholars from Australia and overseas, we run a seminar programme each year at the University of Sydney, and we publish books based on issues raised at the conference. These books include *Words and Worlds, Feudalism,* and *Semiotics, Ideology, Language.*

Our new series, Working Papers, provides pre-publication for research in progress and publishes occasional papers presented at our seminars. We also publish an annual Newsletter for members in order to disseminate information about research in progress, forthcoming conferences, etc.

Inquiries about these publications should be addressed to;

Professor Michael Allen
Department of Anthropology
University of Sydney,
Sydney NSW 2006

Typeset and Printed by Meglamedia
6A Nelson Street, Annandale NSW 2038
Phone (02) 519 1044, Fax (02) 550 3090